PROMISES
TO
KEEP

~ *A Daily Devotional* ~

PROMISES
TO
KEEP

DERICK BINGHAM

Ambassador

DEDICATION

This book is dedicated to Mr. Norrie Watts who, as no other, taught me the beauty and power of words. As Walt Whitman would have said: "Oh! Captain, my captain!"

ACKNOWLEDGEMENTS

I wish to thank my longsuffering secretary, Mrs. Deirdre Cousins for her patient work in staying with this book until the last proverb was commented on. She received 'copy' from the literal ends of the earth and patiently and cheerfully saw it through to the publisher's hands.

Front cover photograph of Julie, Stephanie and Lisa Robinson of "Meadowview Farm", Co. Armagh is by David Graham, A.B.I.P.P., The Studio, Hillsborough, Co. Down. Used by kind permission.

Photograph of author by Andrew Towe.

INTRODUCTION

Promises. Some are made on the spur of the moment, some are forced from us, some are forgotten, some are kept. Any way you look at it we all make promises.

God makes promises too and he never forgets to keep them. They are eternal and guaranteed. To read them, to believe them makes life worth living. They add meaning to the nitty gritty of everyday life. They bring hope and warning, comfort and challenge. A lot of them are found in the great wisdom book of the Bible, the book of Proverbs.

The book of Proberbs has a lot to say about the issues of life. If we would heed its wisdom it would not only change our hearts it would also transform our whole quality of life. Here is instruction for young people in a world where subtle and restless efforts are made to poison their hearts and pervert their ways. here are verbal gold vaults of wisdom for parents raising a family. Here are guidelines for people running an expanding business. Here are words of advice for those who are unemployed and living from hand to mouth. Here is incisive warning about the power of speech. here you will read of advice regarding anger, education, food, greed, justice, self-control, violence, the place of a woman and the place of a man in society and much more.

Join me in a years readings in this most practical of Bible books. As we study it together may we see new promises to keep and learn to trust a God who never fails to keep his.

The woods are lovely, dark and deep,
But I have promises to keep,
And miles to go before I sleep,
And miles to go before I sleep.

- ROBERT FROST

JANUARY

By my fireside is a little statement written in poker work on wood which a friend bought for me in Austria. It reads "If your heart is cold this fire will not warm it". Provoking words, yes? I trust you will find in this cold month of January that the Proverbs from the Bible which we have chosen for you will warm your heart. If your heart is freezing cold may they bring a real spiritual thaw.

January 1st

"He who troubles his own house will inherit the wind and the fool will be servant to the wise of heart." Proverbs 11:29

Martha Mitchell's famous novel about the impermanence of wealth and society was succinctly named "Gone with the Wind". Here, though, is a wind which will wreck more havoc in our homes than a Civil War. It is guaranteed if any member of the family sets out to cause trouble in their own house.

Don't speak roughly today to your wife or husband or you will inherit a wind which will whip happiness out of your intimacy. Don't cut up rough with your parents in case a howling wind of regret haunt you when they are gone. If you have a hell-spark of jealousy or envy against any member of your own family and you don't put it out in a sea of prayer, a wind will come and fan that spark into a flame which will consume you and not them.

On this very first day of the new year make an excellent resolution; be wise of heart and determine never to start trouble in your own home. If you carry out your resolution even fools will do you a good turn.

January 2nd

"Anxiety in the heart of man causes depression, but a good word makes it glad." Proverbs 12:25

You'll not go far into today before you will come across someone who is depressed. Gnawing at their heart will be some anxiety. Money troubles. Family troubles. Hidden illness, maybe, that threatens their very life and has cut down all their plans. You just don't know what is going on deep down in someone's heart. Depression, even in teenagers, is widespread. It is sometimes hidden in a smile that masks a lurking insecurity.

A good word, though, can make a depressed heart glad. Put a few in your quiver and shoot them accurately as you go through the day. I remember speaking at a Convention and quietly hiding anxiety in my heart as I spoke to a listener, after it was all over. "It was my first time to speak on Centre Court", I quipped. "Game, set and match", she said, smiling. My anxiety turned to joy. See what I mean?

January 3rd

"The preparations of the heart belong to man but the answer of the tongue is from the Lord." Proverbs 16:1

Once, in Switzerland, I sat in a radio interview which lasted about two hours. "If you make a mistake", said the lady interviewing me, "it will not be edited. It will go out as a mistake". I shuddered.

Maybe today you have a difficult assignment where you will have to explain yourself. Those shifting feet of yours, that bitten nail, those bags under the eyes, betray worry. You have prepared for the occasion in your heart but you are frightened. Don't be. Why? You and I need to prepare for things and the older I live the more I see that faith breeds organization. Fortune certainly favours the prepared mind. But, when the moment comes to speaking for the Lord, all the preparation in the world will not give you the answer you need to exactly fit the situation as God sees it. That comes from the Lord. Do not fear. He will give you the best answer when you are called to give a reason for the hope that is in you if you trust Him for it. As it turned out, I had a great morning in Geneva!

January 4th

"Bright eyes gladden the heart, good news puts fat on the bones."
Proverbs 15:30

Worry can make you very thin. The flesh sometimes literally walks off people who have frighteningly difficult situations to live through. The haggard sad look dominates many an expression and it certainly takes a worried man to sing a worried song.

But, notice, here comes a little child on to the lap of the worried person. Their little eyes shine with some tale of the wonder they find in what the older person has long since found ordinary. As one word trips out over another, those bright eyes gladden the worried heart.

It is not without significance that the cameras on the television programme "This is Your Life" always concentrate on the smallest child or grandchild present when the credit lines come, as the centre of attraction. Why? Bright eyes gladden the heart.

Did not the Professor tell the children who had been to Narnia that they would be able to discover other people who had a similar experience by the look in their eye?: C. S. Lewis knew all about today's Proverb when he wrote the 'Chronicles of Narnia : Do you? You do? Then show it in your eyes.'

January 5th

"The refining pot is for silver and the furnace for gold, but the Lord tests the hearts." Proverbs 17:3

Recently a new study was made as to why Americans who represent 2% of the world's population consume 60% of the world's illicit drugs. Is there any clue in American culture as to why they use more drugs than anyone else? What's wrong at the heart of such a wealthy nation? "There is no single answer", said a senior official of the Drug Enforcement Administration. "One of the root causes is in the family. Millions of kids are left to themselves and among the poor the single-parent families often just don't function. Among the middle class, mother and father are often too busy with their careers to spare time for the children". A recent study of 5,000 teenage school children in California found that "latch-key children", caring for themselves after school, were twice as likely to use alcohol and 1.7 times as likely to use marijuana as adolescents who grow up under direct adult care.

Those of us who are parents must understand that even if we could afford it, gobs of money at Christmas, expensive holidays, designer clothes or whatever will not substitute for a mother being at home when her child comes home, or a father being constantly and unnecessarily out in the evenings when he should be spending time with his children who will be gone out of his home and life in a shorter time than he ever imagines. Let the Lord test our hearts on this matter and let's do something about it. Pronto.

"Apply your heart to discipline, and your ears to words of knowledge." Proverbs 23:12

My friend Randal Palmer, a journalist on mainland Europe kindly keeps an envelope in his desk. Into it he puts titbits which he feels may be of interest and passes them on to me. They are gold dust. Try this one, called the ABCs of christian behaviour. It expounds our proverb for today, perfectly.

"Act instead of argue. Build instead of brag. Climb instead of criticise. Dig instead of depreciate. Encourage instead of envy. Fight instead of fain. Give instead of grumble. Help instead of harm. Invite instead of ignore. Join instead of jeer. Kneel instead of kick. Love instead of lampoon. Move instead of mould. Nurture instead of neglect. Obey instead of object. Pray instead of pout. Qualify instead of quit. Rescue instead of ridicule. Shout instead of shriek. Try instead of tremble. Undergird instead of undermine. Vindicate instead of vilify. Witness instead of wilt. Exhault instead of excuse. Yield instead of yell. Zip instead of zigzag".

Have a good day!

"Before destruction the heart of a man is haughty, but humility goes before honour." Proverbs 18:12

1989 was a year which expounded this proverb before the eyes of millions. In December 1989 the New York Hotel Queen, Leona Helmsley went into a courtroom a billionaire and emerged a common criminal. The judge ordered her to jail for four years and fined her 7.1 million dollars for seeking to evade taxes on everything from personal clothing to a million dollar marble dance floor and the 130,000 dollar stereo system. Her lawyer asked the judge not to jail her but to let her work at a centre that cared for babies born with drug addition and AIDS. He described this as an environment which would "humble her on a daily basis". It was corrupted capitalism at its worst.

In the very same month a tyrants megalomania was exposed in Europe at the Palace of the People in Bucharest. Built on the orders of President Ceausescu it turned out to be a monumental folly to stupid pride. While the people he was supposed to represent lived in direst poverty with just barely enough to eat he built a palace containing, by some counts, 7,000 rooms including display cases full of cocktail shakers that lit up and played tunes! It was corrupted Communism at its worst. One journalist when he got into the Palace with the revolutionary troops sat down at the grand piano and played a spirited rendition of "As Time Goes By". It was most appropriate.

Read today's proverb once more. Try to memorise it through the day. Obey, by God's grace, its precept and honour will be yours.

January 8th

"All the days of the afflicted are evil, but he who is of a merry heart has a continual feast.' Proverbs 15:15

A bad conscience is a constant affliction. Selfishness brings afflictions which sting like nettles. Pride comes before the affliction of a fall. Jealousy is as cruel as the grave and afflicts all who allow it to rise in their hearts. A godless life brings evil days as sure as a bug brings an epidemic."But he who is of a merry heart has a continual feast", says the proverb. Those who know and follow the Lord have a happiness beyond measure. The longest feast in the Bible lasted for six months (Esther chapter 1) but it had to stop! The joy of the Lord though, is something you can know constantly and it never palls, or sickens, or dissipates. Never. Give thanks to God today, christian, who always causes you to triumph in Christ.

January 9th

"As in water face reveals face, so the heart of man reveals man.'
Proverbs 27:19

Do you ever go through a crowd and catch a snippet of conversation? You know, the smart young fellow says to his girl, as they pass you on the busy street, "I promise you I will never say ..." That's all you hear and you wonder what he'll never say! Why, here are two ladies going by and at every word a reputation dies!

As in water a face is revealed so the things people say reveals what is in their hearts. Listen to them! "Out of the abundance of the heart the mouth speaks", said the Lord Jesus. If we only realised how much our tongues reveal our hearts we would be very careful about what we say. Of course, if we dwell deep with God the overflow is going to constantly seep into our conversations. "The mouth of the righteous is a fountain of life", says the Bible. So, let's ask the question as you pass through the first month of the year, "Is your mouth a fountain or a babbling brook?"

January 10th

"Ointment and perfume delight the heart and the sweetness of the man's friend does so by hearty counsel.' Proverbs 27:9

I have a friend who had us all falling about the other night with a story of an incident in her life. She lifted what she thought was a beautifully packaged perfume called "Romantique" and sprayed it in a few strategic spots to brighten up her day. Later she said to her husband, "I'm coming out in this strange rash on my skin!".

She investigated and to her dismay discovered that "Romantique" was not a perfume but it was a "Spices of Christmas" air freshener! As it turned out the name on the imagined perfume was "Aromatique"!

Room fresheners aside, perfumes certainly delights any heart! Millions of pounds are spent to acquire their delights and no merchandise is more carefully and tastefully packaged. But, think of it; a bit of helpful advice wrapped up with plenty of heart and given to your friend today will be as perfume to his or her heart. What's more, it will be free and if spiritually and biblically based, will last much longer than any perfume. Make sure, of course, that it is a "perfumed-advice" because God knows we have too much advice around that brings on a lot of rashes.

January 11th

"He who trusts in his own heart is a fool, but whoever walks wisely will be delivered." Proverbs 28:26

You cannot trust your heart, it is too devious. It will argue this way this morning and that way tonight. It makes a case for "yes" this minute and "no" next minute. It is an impostor, an adverturer, a boaster, a bluffer, a pretender. It has tried to deceive you from the moment you first drew breath. In it is the seed of every sin of which a human being is capable.

Follow your heart and you will bring burdens into your life which will break you. Put confidence in your heart and you will be filled with disappointment before you are through. But put your confidence in the Lord and what will happen? His yoke is easy and his burden is light. So, quit the calls of the heart for wheeling, dealing and social climbing; get your eye on the Lord and your feet will follow in a path of deliverance and incalculable blessing.

January 12th

"The tongue of the righteous is choice silver; the heart of the wicked is worth little." Proverbs 10:20

"Copy watch! Copy watch, sir!" They were about the most frequent words I heard when in Singapore! Everywhere, I met people touting copies of the most famous brand name watches in the world and few there are who could spot the difference between the copy and the real thing. But the real thing is the choice thing. Choice silver and a cheap version is soon discovered by the eye of the expert.

Learn it well that knowing and following the Lord will affect the quality of words you use. Those who deliberately count Him worthless in their hearts will find their words are soon cast aside. So, let's ask ourselves a simple question: "What value is put on my words?" Choice silver? Worthless? It's a sobering question.

January 13th

"Who can say, 'I have made my heart clean, I am pure from my sin?'" Proverbs 20:9

A christian leader once met a man who told him he hadn't sinned for a considerable length of time. The problem was the same man was driving the leader on the motorway at above the speed limit!

In another incident a christian was cutting another christian's hair and at the same time propounding the theory that he believed himself to be sinlessly perfect. His customer didn't agree with him and the hairdresser got so angry that he almost prematurely balded his customer! His customer, a pastor, said that he was almost afraid to appear in public for about a fortnight! He later commented that if the hairdresser, who thought himself a sinlessly perfect barber, had cut him so sharply what would he not have done to him if he had believed himself to be a sinful barber? No one can say "I am pure from my sin". All of us sin in more ways than we ever even stop to think of. There is only one source of cleansing and the Apostle John put it perfectly when he wrote "The blood of Jesus Christ, His Son, cleanses us from all sin". The lovely fact is that the blood of the Saviour shed at Calvary cleanses us from the guilt of our sin. On top of that, as we pass through a very impure world, the Word of God also continues to cleanse our feet and hands from the defilement they pick up along the way. Read it. Often.

January 14th

"Every way of a man is right in his own eyes but the Lord weighs the hearts." Proverbs 21:2

If there is one trait in human nature which is common to us all it is the difference by which we judge the same action in others and then in ourselves. It is alright for us to do something but let someone else do it and see what we will say about them! Let us be reminded that the Lord ponders and weighs our hearts. He knows how we truly are and what the motivation is for our actions. If you had heard James and

John say "Lord, do you want us to command fire to come down from heaven and consume them, just as Elijah did?", you would have thought them the most pious of fellows. The plain fact was that their motivation was downright religious bigotry. They had gone to a village of the Samaritans to prepare for Christ's entry into it but the Samaritans didn't want Him. Sectarian hatred of the Samaritans was the motivation for the disciples zeal and the Lord detested it. "You do not know what manner of spirit you are of", he said, rebuking them, "For the Son of Man did not come to destroy men's lives but to save them".

As we pass through the day let us constantly, by God's grace, check our motivations.

January 15th

"He who loves purity of heart and whose speech is gracious, the king is his friend." Proverbs 22:11

Gracious words. Pick a few and hand them out today. They will last longer in people's hearts than jewellery or flowers, I can tell you. You think I am speaking unreal talk?

A New England farmer by the name of Luke Short reached 100 years of age fit and well and was sitting in his field meditating one day when he suddenly remembered a sermon that John Flavell had preached 85 years earlier in Dartmouth, England before Luke Short had left for America. As he turned Flavell's words over in his mind they came to him with such power that he was converted on the spot! The gracious words of the Gospel have long life. They are seed that may take a long time to surface but, mark my words, surface they will. Sow plenty today.

"Like one who takes away a garment in cold weather, and like vinegar on soda, is one who sings songs to a heavy heart.'
Proverbs 25:20

When you meet a bereaved person or a troubled heart be careful what you say. More often than not it is better to say very little. Just be there to help and encourage. As Shakespeare put it in Macbeth Act V.iii,

"Cans't thou not minister to a mind diseased,
Pluck from the memory a rooted sorrow,
Raze out the written troubles of the brain,
And with some sweet oblivious antidote,
Cleanse the stuff'd bosom of that perilous stuff,
Which weighs upon the heart?"

The longer I live the more I've come to realise that the best way to help the troubled heart is not to sing it songs but to listen to it speak. Listen and empathise and you will always be welcome.

"Do not let your heart envy sinners, but in the fear of the Lord continue all day long." *Proverbs 23:17*

It's easy to envy people who defy God and His word. Many of them blaspheme and nothing happens to them. No lightning strikes their lifestyle. Many of them cheat in their business lives and instead of making less money they make more. The more wrong they get into the healthier, happier and more successful they seem to be.

Perhaps you have sought to put God first in your life and your business has collapsed, recently. Perhaps you put God first but that has certainly not prevented the sickness or death of your child. You are maybe wondering, today, what it's all about.

I've met faithful christians who have been sorely tempted to quit because of the envy they have of sinners lifestyle. If you are tempted in this area let me ask you one thing. What do you owe to the world, the flesh and the devil? Did they bring you a moments peace in your life? You know where those three lead, don't you? To hell itself. So what are you envying sinners for? Heed today's proverb and live through it in the fear of the Lord. And be careful what television programmes you watch before the day is out. Most films glamorize sin and it's easy to believe them. Let the fear of the Lord control your eyes, too. It will remind you that the wages of sin is death but the gift of God is eternal life through Jesus Christ our Lord.

January 18th

'There are many plans in a man's heart, nevertheless the Lord's counsel - that will stand.' Proverbs 19:21

We all have our plans. Plans for a new business? Family? A holiday? A project? We discuss it. We talk to people of experience. We take counsel. The sad thing is, though, our counsel can be desperately wrong. The British at Singapore expected the Japanese to attack from the sea. Their counsel advised them to point their guns in that direction. I visited one of those gun positions and certainly nothing could have moved above the surface of the water without it being covered. The only problem was the Japanese came on their bicycles from behind and the city fell. In peace and war the best of advice can be wrong.

But the Bible? Never. Listen to it. Obey it. It is the Lord's counsel to you for your life. It will stand. I mean where are those Roman Emperors that thought the gospel a minnow in the river of history? Who are the minnows, of history, now?

January 19th

"A prudent man conceals knowledge but the heart of fools proclaims foolishness." Proverbs 12:23

"I always speak my mind", says the fool. You would think, though, with some folk, that always speaking their mind was a virtue. There are things in our minds we would be far better concealing and our ignorance of certain matters will only be displayed if we talk about them. Even if we have knowledge there is a time and a place to speak of it and a time and a place to conceal it.

"Is your roof isolated?", a man once asked me. He was displaying his ignorance of roof insulation! "I'll be in the hands of the atheist", said an Ulster woman displaying her ignorance of the honourable profession of a hospital anesthetist! "What is wrong with you folk is your environmentals", said a speaker I know of stretching for a bridge to folks minds! As they say in Glasgow of pretentious talk, "Aw! His heid is full of broken bottles".

In Belfast they would degrade such a fool by an even more derogatory expression. They would say "Away home! His head's full of sweety mice!"

Better, is it not, to be thought a fool than to open your mouth and remove all doubt.

January 20th

"A merry heart makes a cheerful countenance, but by sorrow of the heart the spirit is broken." Proverbs 15:13

"The unconverted folk around us are often calm and contented", said a wise lady recently "and we christians are always telling them that they will have peace and joy and contentment if they become christians, and, just look at us!"

Too right. Many a christian has a stomach like a tumble drier and is rushing about frantically from responsibility to responsibility. Just hold on a minute, christian. Did your Lord not say that "His yoke is easy and his burden is light?" Got it? Am I blind or do I really read those two words right; "easy", "light"?

Goodness, to look at some folks expressions it is quite obvious that their hearts are burdened down with sorrows and burdens they have brought on themselves by taking on the yokes that other people want to put on them.

Enough is enough. Wrench those miserable yokes off your heart and life today. Start getting the little word "no" into your vocabulary. The result? A cheerful countenance. After all, the most important thing you will wear today is the expression on your face.

January 21st

"Those who are of a preverse heart are an abomination to the Lord but such as are blameless in their ways are his delight.'
Proverbs 11:20

To bring home a present for someone you love and see them delight in it is a delight in itself. To do something to cheer someones day, to have someone truly glad to see you, makes any old mediocre day suddenly sing and life seem worth living.

But, to bring delight to God? Me? What I do? It is a staggering thought. Yet, when I do that which is right, that which is sincere and true I bring delight to Him. Imagine having a life which is God's delight! What is an Oscar or an

Emmy, a Nobel Prize or some earthly medal of honour in comparison to pleasing God? A perverse heart, though, is an abomination to the Lord. What is perversity? It is self will in the heart, a stubbornness, a determination to have my own way. I often think of the three young men who walked loose with the Lord in the firey furnace. They had been cast into the furnace bound but because of their obedience to God they were set free in their firey trial to walk closer with God. So it will be in any firey trial you pass through for the Lord's sake today. Do not be stubborn but submit to His will. It will bring delight to God and freedom to you.

January 22nd

"Hope deferred makes the heart sick, but when the desire comes it is a tree of life." Proverbs 13:12

Expectations! You hoped for so much from that holiday. Your heart was set on marrying that man. You worked so hard for that exam, day and night and weekends too. You expected so much from that local church you joined. That neighbourhood you moved into recently looked, at last, like your Shangri La.

The holiday was a nightmare. The man married someone else. You failed the exam. The local church became your local heartbreak. The neighbourhood was no brotherhood. Lesson? Cut down on your expectations. Be more realistic.

If my memory serves me right when John Newton went to Cheltenham on the strength of the verse where God had said to Paul that he had "Much people" in the city of Antioch, Newton said he was not long in Cheltenham until he discovered that Cheltenham was not Antioch and he was not Paul!

Don't indulge too deeply in expectations for it brings a borrowed pleasure on which you will have to pay a very high

26

interest. Christian hope is not hope-so. "Blessed are those who hunger and thirst for righteousness for they shall be filled", said the Lord Jesus. That is an expectation which will never disappoint you. Go for it!

January 23rd

"Even in laughter the heart may sorrow, and the end of mirth may be grief.' Proverbs 14:13

"We grin when asked 'How do you do?'
And answer, 'Fine! And what about you?'
But when they ask as to how we are,
Would telling them be going too far?
Well, last night there was a leak in the roof,
And Mary was up with an aching tooth,
And Paul had tears with an ugly sum,
And the fraction also upset his mum.
'How do you do?', I hear you ask,
Well, the mortgage is proving a difficult task,
And the neighbour's dog is under the weather,
Minus an ear because of our setter.
And, my, the fridge no longer freezes,
The spin-drier's been making ugly wheezes,
And, come to think of it, did you know,
The immersion heater's beginning to go?
And since we're talking, it's sad to tell,
Our house we may very soon have to sell,
The cost of living is getting worse,
It's eating a hole in our family purse.
Oh!, I'm sorry, sir, if you have to go,
"Business is pressing?", I know, I know,
But you did ask as to how we were,
And I thought to tell you was only fair."

27

"The backslider in heart will be filled with his own ways but a good man will be satisfied from above.' Proverbs 14:14

All over the nation you will find people who once walked closely with God. Then, Satan arose and set all kinds of traps in their way. They met a hypocrite and Satan whispered "They're all really hypocrites". They found the christian life was a battle against sin but Satan made sin so attractive. They succumbed to his wiles and followed idols of materialism, of social position, of popularity with the crowd. What is the result?

These people become what the Bible calls backsliders and when you talk to them you find they are filled with their own ways. They seldom speak of the Saviour they loved and no longer read His word as they did or speak to Him much in prayer. Their talk is of "me, my and mine" and they are very unhappy. But note christians who walk closely with God; the springs of their satisfaction are in God. Theirs is the true reward. In which category of today's proverb are you? Selah.

"My son, keep your father's command, and do not forsake the law of your mother. Bind them continually upon your heart; tie them around your neck.' Proverbs 6:20,21

I lost my father when I was but a child so I can only speak from experience of my mother. Again and again, all through my childhood and even in college days she would keep reminding me that God had said in His word "Them that honour me I will honour". That was her watchword, a law of her life.

Life has moved on and often, in all kinds of circumstances that little watchword of my mother's surfaces in my mind. Could it be that today you will be faced with a situation where you will be tempted to "play down" the fact that you are a christian?

I plead with you not to be ashamed of your Lord; you have absolutely no reason to be ashamed of Him. After all, He was not ashamed of us when he had every reason to be. Take your stand for Him today and you will find that if you honour Him He will surely honour you. My mother told me so.

January 26th

'The wise in heart will be called prudent, and sweetness of the lips increases learning.' Proverbs 16:21

There is no doubt that wisdom of heart or, God given commonsense, will give you discernment in life. The wiser you become the more you can see a fool for what he is and shady deals for what they are. You will be able to know certain roads in life are only cul-de-sacs and you will save a lot of time and energy by not having to try them.

Our proverb links wisdom of heart with the fact that "sweetness of the lips increases learning". What does this mean? It means that people are better won with honey than vinegar. If you have wisdom in your heart then out of the abundance of your heart your mouth speaks. A flowing style, clear, helpful, winsome expressions easily communicate knowledge and truth.

So, what has been on your lips recently, honey or vinegar? Your answer will prove what condition your heart is in.

"A haughty look, a proud heart and the ploughing of the wicked is sin." Proverbs 21:4

On the surface this is not an easy proverb to understand but a little thought will soon show the treasure in it.

How can ploughing soil, which is a legitimate duty, become a sin? It has to do with motive. People who plough their soil, or do their work, acknowledging God in their work, bring glory to God. Those who do not have any regard for God in their work whatsoever have a corrupt principle which defiles their very best action.

What is life all about. Is life merely to work? Is earning money the meaning to life? Is having a good time the meaning to life? If it is try telling that to someone lying paralysed for 20 years. There's got to be more in life than just working, eating and having a good time. The purpose of life is to bring glory to God.

The underlying motive for what you do in life will affect the look in your eye. Just watch the eyes of those who have no regard for God in what they are doing. There creeps into their eye a very haughty look which comes from a selfish, proud heart. You can tell a lot about a person from the look in their eye. As you go through today be very careful to look to how you look!

"The Lord hates ... a heart that devises wicked plans." Proverbs 6:16

I have lived in a society where at least 30,000 people have been injured as a result of terrorist activity in the past 20 years. Many thousands have died. It is a land of tragic beauty and yet the young people here in Northern Ireland have consistently been getting some of the highest examination results in the United Kingdom in recent years. The flow to Oxford and Cambridge Universities out of Belfast is amazing.

It is a province that has given the world the pneumatic tyre, the aircraft ejector seat, the hydraulic system on tractors, the world's best linen and C. S. Lewis! The list could go on for a long time. I don't know of any society in which I would prefer my children to be raised than in the quality of life found in Northern Ireland. Its beauty is often breathtaking and its people, as any major charity in the United Kingdom will tell you, are consistently amongst the most generous in the nation.

But there are men and women who, every night, sit and plot wickedness against its citizens. They hold a wonderful provinces international image to ransom. While they dominate the news headlines of the world, the vast majority of Northern Ireland's God-fearing citizens are often ignored. To those harassed, but brave and good people I commend today's Proverb. It tells us where the final score lies. Selah.

January 29th

"Wisdom rests quietly in the heart of him who has understanding."
Proverbs 14:33

No one ever spoke like him. Even the people who never spoke to God because they imagined He wouldn't want to know them, found themselves talking to the Saviour. They then discovered he was God and discovered God to be totally different to what they thought he would be. Little children sat on His knee, cheats talked to Him and stopped cheating.

Liars stopped lying, beggars stopped begging, thieves stopped stealing, selfish people became kind and generous, lives were literally transformed. When Christ rests in your heart you then have the Wisdom of God resting in your heart (1 Corinthians 1:24). It is a very precious gift to have. I have watched it display itself in the lives of people who you would never imagine would have ever got to possessing it. It can be yours by trusting Christ. If you have the gift, be glad of it and may the very wisdom of God be seen in your every move, today.

January 30th

"Trust in the Lord with all your heart and lean not to your own understanding; in all your ways acknowledge Him and He shall direct your paths." Proverbs 3:5-6

This is the polar-star of every christian. Lean to yourself, to your own notions and hunches and you will be flotsum and jetsum on life's rivers. Learn to lean on Christ and you will make successful decisions and have a contented journey. And remember, you will never have to regret praying too much over any step you may take.

If Lot had only prayed about the matter he would never have been compromised in Sodom. If Orpah had only prayed about her situation she would never have gone back to Moab. If David had only acknowledged the Lord he never would have gone down to Nob and dozens of men would never have been lost as a result of his lack of trust in the Lord. Make the Lord your counsellor and not your heart. Your life will then be marked by one of the loveliest expressions any christian could make; "I, being in the way the Lord led me". And remember the verse says, "In all your ways acknowledge Him". All your ways means in everything; personal, public, private, temporal, eternal. You will never be disappointed by a refusal of guidance from God. So, just now, ask God for that guidance and you will be amazed what will transpire before the day is through.

January 31st

"Give me your heart, my son and let your eyes delight in my ways."
Proverbs 23:26

There are many who make claim to your heart. If Satan would try to capture the Saviour's heart, would he not try to capture yours?

Notice that Satan did not say to the Lord "Sing me a few choruses in my honour" or "Have strong feelings of emotion toward my greatness". Notice that he said "All these things I will give you if you will fall down and worship me". There is more to worship than feeling and singing. There is an emphasis on falling down. Why?

Worship has to do with answering the question "Who really owns me? Who is the ultimate authority in my life?" Is money, or honour, or pleasure, or academic learning, or social position the thing that owns you? Do you bow down to it? If you do it will have your heart and God despises a divided heart.

Notice that in this Proverb God does not ask for pompous ceremony or a magnificent building. He does not say "Give me your home" or "Give me your money" or "Give me your ambitions", or even, "Give me your hands, or feet or tongue". He simply asks for the moving principle behind all that we are and do. He says "Give me your heart". Everything hangs on this point. Everything. Give it and incalculable blessing will be yours. Withhold it and incalculable ruin is certain. As you

33

pass through your day sing this addition to the lovely words of the hymn "When I survey the wondrous cross". The additional words are "Love so amazing, so divine, shall have my heart, my life, my all".

FEBRUARY

FEBRUARY

How many a child on a cold February morning has not wanted to face a day at school? They have spoken from beneath warm, cosy blankets of sore stomachs and aching legs but it has not fooled their mothers. Why? Because their mothers have often applied the test of the state of a stomach's health by simply saying, "Show me your tongue!" A coating on the tongue indicates a sickness in the stomach. A clean tongue sends the child to school!

The tongue is a test of spiritual health, too. Let's apply it through February days.

February 1st

"There is one who speaks like the piercings of a sword, but the tongue of the wise promotes health." Proverbs 12:18

How does a mother get her baby to sleep? With her tongue. She sings to it. How do counsellors comfort depressed individuals? With their tongues. With kind words. How do ambassadors adequately represent nations? By diplomatic speech. How do teachers coax a backward pupil forward? By using encouraging language. The health of a nation, a city, a village or a home is promoted by wise words.

Sadly a lot of people have no notion of the power of the words they use. They often say just whatever comes into their heads and don't realise that the words they are using are as a sword in their hand. They stab and pierce with sarcasm and unremitting "cattiness" and leave deeply wounded lives behind.

Bring healing with your words today. If we all reviewed the words we are about to use in our minds before we speak them a lot of doctors clinics would be emptied of people with ulcers, depression, insomnia, eczema and the numerous illnesses and problems brought on by people who say the wrong thing to them. A new health campaign starts on this page this month in this book : its slogan is "wise words promote health".

February 2nd

Righteous lips are the delight of kings, and they love him who speaks what is right.' Proverbs 16:13

I like the translation of this Proverb which reads "Righeous lips are the delight of kings and he who speaks right is loved". Let's, gentlemen, apply it to marriage. Would the following words be frequent in your house?

"Let me open the car door for you". "Those groceries need lifting, let me help". "That meal was delicious". "You always look good but tonight you look terrific." Or, how about the little words like "Please", "I'm sorry", "Thank you", "Forgive me" and, above all, "I love you"?

Remember, "He who speaks what is right is loved". Words, if sincerely meant, gentlemen, transform relationships. And, what's more, they outlast roses and candlelight dinners.

February 3rd

'On her tongue is the law of kindness.' Proverbs 31:26

No, ladies I didn't forget you. Yesterday's message was for the men, today's is for you!

Sarah used manipulative words to move Abraham into accepting surrogate motherhood and as a result we have the Arab-Israeli conflict to this day. Rebecca talked her son into deceiving her blind husband and brought sorrows upon her head. A clever talking widow persuaded David into allowing the scoundrel Absalom back into his court and David lost his throne. Sweet talking women turned the wise Solomon's head and he became an effeminate fool.

The woman in Proverbs was different. In her tongue was the law of kindness. A law is to be obeyed so, obviously, this woman didn't let a word pass her lips without first asking "Is this word I am about to say, kind?" Apply that law, ladies, and no one will ever be hurt by anything you say.

February 4th

"Wisdom is found on the lips of him who has understanding, but a rod is for the back of him who is devoid of understanding. Wise people store up knowledge, but the mouth of the foolish is near destruction." Proverbs 10:13-14

One Tuesday evening while shaking hands with my Bible Class on their way in to study the Bible on the subject of the tongue, a quiet man handed me a slip of paper. On it were written these words: "You are master of the unspoken word but the spoken word is master of you". The truth of those provoking words is shown very clearly by today's Proverb. A fool says anything that takes his fancy and his words become a rod on his back. They return to haunt him. He lives to regret them for the rest of his life. The wise realise that the spoken word's power is great and since the tongue sits in a wet place and is liable to slip, they use words carefully. Instead of those words coming back to beat them like a rod, the words of the wise enhance, protect, bless and preserve them. Tell me, are your words a rod or a preservative?

February 5th

"A man has joy by the answer of his mouth, and a word spoken in due season, how good it is!" Proverbs 15:23

Sir Winston Churchill was at his most dangerous when he seemed bored. Hunched over in his seat below the gangway a short distance from the Treasury Bench, he would appear to be inattentive to what was going on around him in the House of Commons. He would close his eyes and breathe heavily. It was a trap and two MPs on the opposite side of the House fell into it.

One said, "Must you fall asleep when I am speaking?" Sir Winston replied, "No, it was purely voluntary!" The second thought himself wiser and merely enquired as to whether Churchill was asleep. Sir Winston immediately replied "I wish I were!"

Since the televising of Parliament we have now seen very clearly that the bite of political debate can be amusing, brilliant, spiteful, good, wicked, kind, inspiring, and incredibly dull and depressing all in one afternoon! Yet the message of today's Proverb is that no matter who we are, if we choose a word fitted to and helpful in any situation, it will always be good. Always. Try a few today.

February 6th

"An ungodly man digs up evil, and it is on his lips like a burning fire.' Proverbs 16:27

There is always someone in the community who wants to dig up dirt. You can usually identify them by the little word "but". They sit in company in a home and it is not long before somebody comes up for discussion in the conversation. Notice carefully what the person who digs up dirt says. Their line usually follows a very predictable pattern, like "He's a good businessman, but did you know ...?", or, "She's very intelligent but about a year ago ..." Watch that little word "but".

The evil on such a person's lips is "like a burning fire". I always remember what a policeman said about the Bradford football stadium disaster. "The fire", he said, "went faster than a man can run". The same happens to the words of a digger of evil. Don't pass on his "buts".

February 7th

'A perverse man sows strife, and a whisperer separates the best of friends". Proverbs 16:28

When you want to whisper something, ask yourself "Why do I want to whisper this?". The simple reason usually is that there is something you don't want someone to hear, else you wouldn't be whispering. In that simple fact lies the destructive power whisperers have in separating the best of friends.

Jim Vaus, America's famous wiretapper was converted to Christ and once demonstrated our Proverb. He stood up in a christian service and told how he had set up some hidden tape recorders at the back of the church building as the people had been coming in. He said he would play them at a later service. It is not surprising to discover that he was actually approached by men after the service offering him money! As it turned out he had forgotten to switch the tape recorders on!

God's recorder is always switched on. Selah.

February 8th

"He who goes about as a tale-bearer reveals secrets: therefore do not associate with one who flatters with his lips". Proverbs 20:19

There are two people in our Proverb. The first is a gossip and the second is a flatterer. What is the difference?

Flatterers are people who say things to your face that they would never say behind your back and gossipers are those

41

who say behind your back the things that they would never say to your face. Give both the flatterer and the gossip a wide berth.

February 9th

'He who passes by and meddles in a quarrel not his own is like one who takes a dog by the ears." Proverbs 26:17

If you go along the road today and catch a dog by the ears you'll create a lot of noise and be fortunate to get away with your arm intact. You could lose a lot more than your arm if you meddle in a quarrel that isn't your own. Wisdom often dictates neutrality when it comes to other people's quarrels. "Get stuck in" and there's every possibility you'll get struck out.

You want an example of wise neutrality? "Teacher", said a man to the Lord Jesus, "tell my brother to divide the inheritance with me". But the Lord Jesus said to him "Man, who made me a judge or an arbitrator over you?" He then left him with a good word but did not in any way meddle in the quarrel the man had with his brother. He knew what taking the dog by the ears would bring. So should we.

February 10th

"He who sends a message by the hand of a fool cuts off his own feet and drinks violence. Like the legs of the lame that hang limp is a proverb in the mouth of fools. Like one who binds a stone in a sling is he who gives honour to a fool. Like a thorn that goes into the hand of a drunkard is a proverb in the mouth of fools.'
Proverbs 26:6-9

I have watched them, often. I have burned inside as they

have operated. It would break your heart. Some public occasion is in hand, a marriage reception, a business promotion, an important family gathering and a fool is honoured by being given something important to say. The results are graphically described in our Proverb.

So, you don't want to embarrass the fool by not giving him something important to do? I solemnly warn you that if you give it to him you'll be the embarrassed one. God knows I've proved it. It will only bring disgust. It is no more fitting for a fool to meddle with intelligent speech than for a drunken man to handle a thorn bush. Give trustworthy work to trustworthy people.

February 11th

"It is honourable for a man to stop striving, since any fool can start a quarrel." Proverbs 20:3

"Try to keep away from pressure", the surgeon told me. I'm sure he was absolutely right in his advice but I find that it would be as easy to keep away from life as it would to keep away from pressure! Deadlines, schedules, commitments, people's problems; the pressures build up, don't they? It seems to me you'd need to go to the moon, virtually, to get away from pressure but even there you would need oxygen to keep you from the pressure that would kill you in seconds!

We certainly need to keep away from pressure points which will affect our health but according to our Proverb we also need to seek to keep away from strife. In fact the parable tells us it is a very honourable thing for anybody to avoid striving. Any fool can start a quarrel but make sure as you pass through today that you are nobody's fool. It takes two to quarrel. Do the honourable thing and put a guard on your tongue when a potential quarrel arises. There are plenty of couples who will

43

have a blazing quarrel today and if you ask them next week they won't be able to tell you what started it. Let's be careful. Silence, you know, is a very hard thing to quarrel with. Remember that!

February 12th

"The mouth of the righteous is a fountain of life." Proverbs 10:11

I was in the little town of Parhead near Edinburgh and the children of the Humbie community nearby had prepared a lovely reception for me including the most delightful coffee and scones. The building where I was treated so warmly was a converted supermarket and included a video room where special tables and headsets were available. Anyone could come in off the street and watch a very large selection of christian teaching and preaching on video. It was all the result of some very hard work by some very dedicated christian people. Visit it, sometime, and see it for yourself.

At the back of the building is a famous local spring which my friends have utilized and piped into the front of the coffee lounge and video room where the water cascades down a specially placed rock. By it is a video recorder playing a tape featuring a christian soloist singing the hymn "I'm drinking at the springs of living water!" I smiled when I saw it. If you have tasted of Christ, the fountainhead, then He says the water which He gives you will become in you "A fountain of water springing up into everlasting life". Will there be any evidence of that fountain in your life today?

February 13th

"The wise in heart will be called prudent, and sweetness of the lips increases learning." Proverbs 16:21

It is worth recognizing that when you issue a reckless statement you never improve any relationship. Such language neither clarifies any issue nor strengthens any relationship.

If you have recently been abusing someone with the needle in your tongue, tell me, is the reaction after you have used the needle one of openness and the desire to discuss the situation or is it one of anger and silence? Are you any further on as a result?

Sweetness of speech increases learning and understanding. It is far more persuasive. The Proverb is not saying we must use insincere language but a few kind and pleasant words would have been far more helpful than your recent diatribe. Take the needle out of your tongue and swap it for a few sugar cubes.

February 14th

'He who has a deceitful heart finds no good, and he who has a perverse tongue falls into evil." Proverbs 17:20

Sitting one day in my favourite eating place, the one and only Red Fox Coffee Shop in one of Northern Ireland's most beautiful villages, Hillsborough, a waitress came storming by, very annoyed about something. I have laughed over it many a time since.

What had happened was that a lady had ordered a baked potato. But she had not only ordered a potato she had insisted it must be a round potato! As the waitress came past she looked at me in despair asking "What did she expect, a square one?"

Some people do have a twisted sense of things. Let's get a balance into our thinking and stop making silly demands.

"As a rule man's a fool,
When it's hot he wants it cool,
When it's cool he wants it hot,
Always wanting what it's not."

February 15th

"He who answers a matter before he hears it, it is folly and shame to him." Proverbs 18:13

Mr. Bob Jordan, Director of the Northern Ireland Chamber of Commerce and Industry tells the story of the farmer who wanted to borrow a tractor from another farmer. As he went up the long lane to his neighbour's farm the farmer began to worry as to how he would ask for the tractor. In his mind he tried this way and that and got very uptight about it all. Eventually he got to the door of the neighbouring farmer's house, highly agitated. When the farmer answered his knock, he burst out "Aw! Just keep your old tractor!"

Read today's Proverb again.

February 16th

"Pleasant words are a honeycomb, sweet to the soul and healing to the bones." Proverbs 16:24

Inspiration! That's what we need. Life is hard. Times are tough. All of us face heartaches and seemingly insurmountable problems. Let us just remind ourselves that our tongues could bring healing and inspiration wherever we go today.

All around you are people who honestly feel sick in their hearts with guilt because of things they have said and done. But, please, remember, you can't see a person's soul and life saved by just telling them of their sins. They know them too well already. Tell them that there is pardon and love waiting for them in Christ. When you meet a wrecked life tell the person you believe in them and never give up.

When Mrs. Gibson gave us pure honey right from the honeycomb out of the hive at the bottom of her garden in Newcastle, Co. Down, as lads, we came back for more. Could you blame us?

February 17th

"Whoever guards his mouth and tongue keeps his soul from troubles." Proverbs 21:23

Robert Morris was a 24 year old graduate student who jammed a nationwide system of thousands of computers with a devastating "worm" program. Computer experts who analysed Morris's program and files say they believe he intended the worm to harmlessly inhabit different computers, possibly flashing a message to alert users to security "holes", but a small error made it reproduce uncontrollably, clogging every machine it entered. At the time of writing Morris faces up to five years imprisonment and a fine of $152,500. Such "hacking" can have devastating consequences for all of us who use computers.

Even more danagerous is the unguarded word. A computer worm can wipe out files and priceless information but the worm of an unguarded word can crawl through a community, city or nation and wipe out lives. Let it loose and you'll not need to go looking for trouble. Trouble will come looking for you.

February 18th

"He who rebukes a man will find more favour afterwards than he who flatters with the tongue.' Proverbs 28:23

If this Proverb is true then what I am going to do to you for a few days is for your good. Recently I was really challenged regarding my lifesytle by a series of questions derived from the BUPA Manual of Fitness and Wellbeing. I was not flattered by my score and you might not be either, but it might do you good. Here are the questions for the section "Do you display symptoms of stress?" Tick all those to which you would answer "yes".

1. Do you often want to cry?
2. Do you bite your nails, fidget with your feet or twiddle your hair?
3. Are you indecisive?
4. Do you feel that there's nobody you can talk to?
5. Are you often irritable and unsociable?
6. Do you eat when you aren't hungry?
7. Do you feel you can't cope?
8. Do you sometimes feel so tense that you think you'll explode, or do you have explosive rages?
9. Do you drink or smoke to calm your nerves?
10. Are you an insomniac?
11. Are you gloomy and suspicious of the motives of others?

If you answer "yes" to more than four of the questions, you are over-stressed and should do something to alleviate it by changing the way you live. Your doctor will give you advice and, if need be, short-term treatment.

February 19th

"Idle chatter leads only to poverty". Proverbs 14:23

The following is not idle chatter. Answer each question with either "never", "rarely", "sometimes" or "often".

1. Do your emotions run away with you?

2. Do you try to avoid awkward situations or people?
3. Do you seek approval from everyone you meet?
4. Have you the ability to see yourself as others see you?
5. Do you dread being alone?
6. Do you feel you are no longer in control of your own life?
7. Do you think it is a sign of weakness to feel grief?
8. Do you believe that a perfect relationship is impossible?
9. Do you feel isolated?
10. Do you dislike yourself?
11. Do you feel depressed?
12. Do you feel you have nothing more to contribute?
13. Do you feel that other people are talking about you in an uncomplimentary way?
14. Do you avoid contact with other people?
15. Do you harbour regrets and resentments?

Score 1 for each question that you can answer with "never"; 2 for "rarely"; 3 for "sometimes"; 4 for "often".

If you have scored under 20 you are rational but probably lacking in originality and sparkle. If you have scored 20-30 you are healthy and balanced but possibly inflexible. If you have scored 30-45 you suffer some doubts and dissatisfaction. Accept that none of us is perfect. If you have scored 45-60 you take life too seriously and it is time for a major overhaul of your lifestyle. Such an overhaul will lead to anything but poverty.

February 20th

"A flattering mouth works ruin." Proverbs 26:28

Now for the tough one. These questions certainly will not flatter you, but they might prevent your unnecessary death.

They answer the question "Are you a candidate for a coronary?" Tick all those to which you would answer "yes".

1. Do you have an unremitting urge to compete?
2. Are you easily aroused to anger, irritation and impatience?
3. Are you aggressive with people who get in your way?
4. Do you find it difficult to bear waiting or queues?
5. Do you speak in a loud voice?
6. Do you not only interrupt but finish other people's sentences and even stories for them?
7. Do you smoke?

In the 1960's Friedman and Rosenaman devised a way of classifying personalities. Temperament is related to health; the agressive, highly competive man or woman, labelled Type A by Friedman and Rosenaman is twice as likely to have coronary heart disease as the more passive Type B. If you have answered "yes" to more than half of the questions you are a Type A personality and must learn to relax if you want to maintain your health. You have been warned.

February 21st

"Like a mad man who throws firebrands, arrows and death, is the man who deceives his neighbour, and says, "I was only joking!"
Proverbs 26:18-19

A deranged person is not responsible for his actions but a person who coolly and deliberately deceives someone and then calls it a joke may fool others but will not fool God. Deceivers are accountable to God.

Rather than be friends with some folk it is better to be at variance with them. Again and again, even with practical jokers, things can go wrong. What was meant as a joke can turn into a nightmare.

People who pretend that they are joking while all the t[...]
they are deceiving are lethal. The Proverb speaks of such as
being like those who throw firebrands and shoot arrows. Fire
burns and arrows kill. Watch the joker, he may be covering
a plot to ruin you.

February 22nd

*"Do you see a man hasty in his words? There is more hope for a
fool than for him." Proverbs 29:20*

Some people, when they speak, sound as if they must
overhaul the universe before they finish. They do not allow
for the fact that they could ever be wrong. Even fools are
capable of becoming conscious of their weakness, asking for
help and finding it. Such people are more capable of being
led right than the ones who think themselves right already.

Are you like an Antony who would "Put a tongue in every
wound of Caesar that should move the stones of Rome to rise
and mutiny"? You will even open up fresh wounds with
hasty words. Don't be worse than a fool. Be swift to hear and
slow to speak. Test everything by the standard of God's word
before you make comments. Then your comments will be
much set by.

February 23rd

*'A wholesome tongue is a tree of life, but perverseness in it breaks
the spirit." Proverbs 15:4*

The wedding was different. No other wedding vows I ever
heard of have had included in them the promise that neither
bride nor groom would ever use sarcasm to each other.
Would you have said "yes" if such a vow had been mandatory
in your wedding vows?

51

To pervert means to "twist the meaning of" and sarcasm certainly does that. And is not exaggeration the same? It is seeking to pervert facts to make information more sensational and manipulative. Flattery is in the same league; it is to praise, but to praise too much. Such things can crush the spirit when seen in their true light. May the Lord make our tongues like a tree of life, bringing its seasonal fruit.

Please don't move your tongue to crush anyone's spirit today. Keep it wholesome.

February 24th

"An evil doer gives heed to false lips; a liar listens eagerly to a spiteful tongue." Proverbs 17:4

Jealousy is often at the base of most criticism. It is a rotten sewer pipe in your heart that spews its venom out on the tongue, usually in the form of spiteful words.

Ask God to clean it because once the venom is spoken you will find liars around you only too glad to use it. And, when you think about it, even liars are not the only ones who will twist what you say. At school a teacher once demonstrated this fact for our class. He whispered a statement into a pupil's ear and then the statement was whispered around about two dozen of us. The last person was allowed to speak what he had heard. When our teacher told us what he had originally said you wouldn't have recognised the end result. Don't give fuel to the fires of liars.

February 25th

*'A man will be satisfied with good by the fruit of his mouth and the recompense of man's hand will be rendered to him."
Proverbs 12:14*

A boy was found on a railway station platform weeping. A

gentleman went over to talk to him and discovered that the lad had lost his railway ticket. The gentleman felt it his duty to help him and bought him a ticket on the one condition that whenever the child would one day in his life come across someone in a similar circumstance he would do the same for that person. As the train pulled out of the station the boy leaned out of the window and shouted back to the gentleman "I will pass it on, sir. I promise. I will pass it on". That deed of simple goodness could still be being enacted somewhere in the world today. And so the deed of kindness that you have done could be reverberated in the very same way. Don't neglect to do it.

February 26th

"Better is the poor who walks in his integrity than one who is perverse in his lips, and is a fool." Proverbs 19:1

So, you don't have much money? You feel a failure in comparison to some people around you? But what you have, you earned, honestly. True? It is better for you to be poor and have integrity than for you to be rich and to have your money by perversity.

It is worth remembering that money can buy a house but not a home. It can buy entertainment but not happiness. It can buy medicine but not health. It can buy a bed but not sleep. It can buy you company but not friends. It is, of course, very useful for paying bills with but remember those who want to get rich fall into temptation and a snare and many foolish and harmful desires which plunge people into ruin and destruction. You would be better living with a little money and have integrity and be able to look people straight in the eye than to live in a palace through perversity and have to constantly divert your eyes. Integrity is the thing.

"Do not answer a fool according to his folly, lest you also be like him. Answer a fool according to his folly, lest he be wise in his own eyes." Proverbs 26:4-5

The temptation to answer back is sometimes quite over-whelming, especially when you are talking to fools. Such people are so ridiculous in the things they say it would not be hard, you think, to talk them down. Such thinking is a trap.

Think about Moses. He faced a situation where he was personally blamed for bringing the children of Israel into a waterless wilderness. They told him they would rather be dead. "And why", they asked, "have you made us come up out of Egypt, to bring us to this evil place? It is not a place of grain or figs or vines or pomegranates; nor is there any water to drink". God told Moses to speak "To the rock before their eyes, and it will yield its water; thus you shall bring water for them out of the rock, and give drink to the congregation and their animals". But Moses answered the fools according to their folly and struck the rock twice. God banned him from the Promised Land. Moses came down to the level of the people's folly and the result was disastrous. The answerer became like the fools around him. The principle to follow is to answer a fool as he deserves or he might think himself wise if you come down to his level. Today's Proverb is a very useful little Proverb to tuck into your mind as you go about your business today. This is because there are as many fools around today as ever there were in Moses's time.

"Like an earring of gold and an ornament of fine gold is a wise reprover to an obedient ear." Proverbs 25:12

To make a mistake, to do the right thing the wrong way, to show inexperience and naivety; we have all known these things. The experience of life is often like that of a rabbit in a minefield!

There is, though the one who comes to reprove us, to advise us, to show us a better way. He is called in this Proverb the wise reprover. He comes tactfully and gently, pointing us in the right direction. No gold earring or ornament will ever look better than the combination of obedient listening to wise reproof. Such was Abigail to David as she saved him from murderous activity. Such was Paul to Peter as he saved him from sectarianism. Such was Eli's word to young Samuel which saved him from missing God's voice. Sadly, when Samuel grew and became a wise reprover to Saul he found a disobedient ear. The end was disaster. Has a wise reprover spoken to you this week? Listen to him.

February 29th

"By the blessing of the upright the city is exalted, but it is overthrown by the mouth of the wicked." Proverbs 11:11

The Pastor of a church in Timisoara, Petru Dugulescu tells of extraordinary scenes which followed the carnage of the Securitate clamp down in his city during the recent revolution in Romania.

Days after several members of his congregation were killed by soldiers loyal to Ceausescu, Petru preached to 100,000 people in the main square and led them in the Lord's Prayer. The following day he preached again, this time to a crowd of 200,000. After he had spoken the crowd began to chant "God exists, God exists".

The wicked had overthrown a city but the upright kept going and, suddenly, the truth surfaced. I cannot tell where today's reading is being read but wherever or whoever you are, christian, as we pass out of February days,do not give in to the godless society around you, the truth as it is in Jesus will triumph. Be faithful to it and blessing will follow.If you have anydout about it just ask Petru Dugulescu.

MARCH

Wealth. The ads invite us to holiday in Marbella, to drive an Audi through the mountains, to fax the latest contract to the New York office. The democracy of taste in a culture of mass consumption is aimed at those with a disposable income. It implies everyone drinks Coke and can afford Levi's jeans never to speak of a telephone like Mrs. Jones's by which means she buys the washing machine, the freezer, or, whatever, at the local sale. The ad men say the key to social distinction today is between those who spend time to save money and those who spend money to save time. But what is true wealth? Money? Let's dip into Proverbs and see what it says on the subject. You might be surprised.

March 1st

"It is the blessing of the Lord that makes one rich and he adds no sorrow with it." Proverbs 10:22

All wealth in this world brings headaches. First there is the headache of getting it and then, once you've got it, of hanging on to it. Devaluation or inflation, wrong investment and carelessness can wipe out wealth in a moment.

The blessing of the Lord is so different. Think of the man who wrote today's Proverb. He earned more than £1 million a day and, yet, when the Lord gave him the blessing of wisdom as a gift, God's gift outweighed his money in value by far.

"I also gathered for myself silver and gold and the special treasures of kings and indeed all was vanity and grasping for the wind. There is no profit under the sun", said Solomon. The important thing to note is that there is profit above the

sun, though, isn't there? That's where the sorrowless blessing comes from. Seek it.

March 2nd

"A gracious woman retains honour but ruthless men retain riches."
Proverbs 11:16

No story portrays the truth of this Proverb better than the
story of Esther and Hamman. Hamman was an extremely
wealthy prince in the palace of King Ahasueurus. His
incredible pride was threatened by one man who refused to
bow to him, namely Mordecai, the Jew. The violence that
rose in his heart was frightening; Hamman arranged for every
Jew in 127 provinces from India to Ethiopia to be wiped out
in one day.

In contrast, Esther, the King's outstandingly beautiful wife
loved the Lord and loved her people and exposed the violent
Hamman and gained great blessing for her nation. Her
honour is retained to this day. The lesson is that we must not
be ashamed to take our stand for the Lord even when ruthless
men surround us. Esther stands as a shining beacon of
encouragement.

March 3rd

---

*"Treasures of wickedness profit nothing but righteousness delivers
from death." Proverbs 10:2*

Ill gotten gains profit nothing. They ended in Judas's
suicide. They brought the curse of God on Ahab. What good
did they do for Zacchaeus? They didn't do much for Jacob,
either, for all he could say to Pharaoh when he was an old man
was "Few and evil have been the days of the years of my life".

What a miserable testimony! Only the overriding grace of God saved him.

So it is with all of us. The righteousness of Christ is that which will outlast all the treasures of this world. Are you building the foundation of your life and your eternity on it? If you are you can be certain that you are safe in the hollow of His hand.

March 4th

"He who trusts in his riches will fall but the righteous will flourish like foliage." Proverbs 11:28

I have seen them, these people who trust in riches. There is an arrogance, a lack of humble dependence upon and looking to the Lord in their lifestyle. They are fools because the Scriptures point out that money has eagle's wings. The eagle is the only bird I know of which can take off in a storm with ease.

Let devaluation, or inflation hit the money market and a fortune can disappear with frightening ease. Money now moves from computer to computer at the speed of light. In three minutes the Global money market can trade currency values equivalent to the annual national income of major states. The impermanence of monetary values now pervades the world of money.

Don't, repeat don't trust in riches. Trust in the Lord.

March 5th

"A present is a precious stone in the eyes of its possessor." Proverbs 17:8

I love surprise presents, don't you? They can lift many a weary day, especially if thought has gone into their choosing.

May I be forgiven, but I dislike "soft" presents in coloured paper at Christmas! Why? It usually means socks, a tie or a shirt. These are most useful and are gratefully received but they are not the most original present in the world. Men like surprises too, you know!

Presents are big business around the world. Why? Because they powerfully turn the affection of the receiver to the giver. So it should be with the Lord's gifts to us. Cherish them because the Bible says that God's gifts are without repentance. That means God is never sorry he gave them to us and he won't withdraw them. He holds us responsible, though, for what we do with them. Put God's gifts to good use today.

March 6th

"It is good for nothing", cries the buyer; but when he has gone his way, then he boasts.' Proverbs 20:14

"The horse you slight the most is the one you buy", said my Co.-Donegal-born friend Mr. Joe Morrow as we drove along, one day. "Say that again", I asked. "The horse you slight the most is the one you buy", he repeated. "What do you mean?", I asked.

"Well", said Joe, "at a horse fair a man will walk up and down looking at horses and you will find that the one he criticises most is often the one he is really interested in and buys".

Joe was, in fact, being very scriptural. Our Proverb tells us it is even a trick of buyers to downgrade a bargain in order to secure it for themselves. Then they boast about it. Is someone criticising you and your work? Don't get discouraged. It is a backhanded compliment to you. Keep going, you are going to make an impact at last!

'He who is greedy for gain troubles his own house, but he who hates bribes will live." Proverbs 15:27

You want a graphic illustration of today's Proverb? Try Jeremiah. "As a partridge that broods but does not hatch, so is he who gets riches but not by right; it will leave him in the midst of his days and at his end he will be a fool" (Jeremiah 17:11). You can't get straighter talk about a greedy bribe taker than that, can you?

Perhaps you can! Try Jeremiah 22. "Woe to him who builds his house by unrighteousness ... who uses his neighbours service without wages and gives him nothing for his work, who says 'I will build myself a wide house ... panelling it with cedar'. Shall you reign because you enclose yourself in cedar? Did not your father eat and drink and do justice and righteousness? Then it was well with him. He judged the cause of the poor and needy; then it was well. Was not this knowing me?", says the Lord. Jeremiah certainly understood today's Proverb. Do we?

'The poor man is hated even by his own neighbour, but the rich has many friends." Proverbs 14:20

A friend is one who comes in when the world goes out. God forgive us if our value of a person's worth has to do with their position in life or the wealth they have. Live for the Lord Jesus and use your possessions to further his work. People will find him as a result and those people will then become your eternal friends. You don't believe me? Read Luke 16:1-13, and particularly verse 9. This parable is implying that some will have more friends in Heaven than others. It all depends what you do with your material possessions. I'd rather have eternal friends than the kind the prodigal had in Luke 15, wouldn't you? So, it's up to you.

March 9th

"Honour the Lord with your possessions and with the first fruits of all your increase; so your barns will be filled with plenty and your vats will overflow with new wine." Proverbs 3:9-10

A lot of christians tend to use the words "materialism", "selfishness" and "greed" as being synonymous with wealth creation. Is it right to throw stones at those who create wealth by earning money for their work?

It is often forgotten that the Lord Jesus worked as a carpenter for most of his adult life. Bronze, iron and cattle in the mixed economy of early Genesis are not frowned on. The Good Samaritan had to have money in his wallet in order to help the unfortunate man-by-the-wayside. The Director of the Institute of Directors recently criticised today's modern church because he reckoned it looked upon business and industry as "mucky and squalid".

Today's Proverb shows it is not the Bible's attitude. Earn your money honestly. Give the Lord His due and not only will He bless you, your giving will be a blessing to others.

March 10th

"Where no oxen are, the trough is clean; but much increase comes by the strength of the ox." Proverbs 17:4

There are some church buildings where the carpet never gets soiled by the Dr. Martens of a scruffy teenager. The weekly routine is never spoiled by some young christian rising to pray, in a stumbling way, for the first time. Babies spoil routines, you know; without them everything is clean, but, there is no growth. The church that ignores them will soon die.

Our Proverb is very clear. It is saying that if you want a harvest you will have to work at it and encourage those who help you. It might create a mess for a while but it brings in incalculable blessing. So it is with all evangelism and let's not forget it.

March 11th

"He who tills his land will have plenty of bread but he who follows frivolity will have poverty enough." Proverbs 28:19

Let's face it, left to itself the land is full of brambles, nettles, thorn bushes and thistles; endless weeds will grow without hesitation. Is not life like that? Don't bother about things; let them drift, just take it as it comes, forget about vision and preparation and careful planning and thought and see what happens. Chaos will soon dominate your life. Follow empty pursuits ("frivolity" in our Proverb) and you will have poverty enough and to spare.

Let's heed Paul's word to us all when he said "Not lagging behind in diligence, fervent in spirit, serving the Lord". Just because you have a job doesn't mean you must stop looking for work. As the slogan at IBM says "We're too busy not to see you".

March 12th

"A man with an evil eye hastens after riches and does not consider that poverty will come upon him." Proverbs 28:22

The ancient Israelites were very much into using parts of

the body as metaphors of psychological phenomena of mind, spirit and body. For example they would look upon the kidney as representing motivation in life or the heart as representing understanding. Here in our Proverb a man is said to have an evil eye and this represents an eye which is selfish. He wants riches and he is in a great hurry to get them. His haste will be his undoing for as the man said "People who don't know whether they are coming or going are usually in the biggest hurry to get there".

Lot hastened to Sodom with his eye on merely materialistic gain and he ended up a wretched, degraded, lonely, poverty stricken tenant of a cave in Zoar. His uncle Abraham, though gave what he couldn't keep to gain what he couldn't lose and he was rich beyond measure. Don't be in a hurry to be rich or you will have pleanty of time to reflect on why you aren't.

March 13th

"The name of the Lord is a strong tower; the righteous run to it and are safe. The rich man's wealth is his strong city, and like a high wall in his own esteem." Proverbs 18:10-11

Think of the Lord's name, which is our strong tower. Elohim, the Lord of greatness and glory. El-Shaddi; the Lord who nourishes and satisfies. Adonai; the Lord, my owner. Jireh; the Lord my provider. Rophe; the Lord who heals. Nissi; the Lord my Father. M'Kaddesh; the Lord who satisfies. Shalom; the Lord my peace. Tsidkenu; the Lord my righteousness. Rohi; the Lord my shepherd. Shammah; the Lord who is there.

Now I know money is useful, particularly to a homemaker who has to push a trolley around a supermarket at £100 an hour! I know money is like digging with a needle and spending it, for all of us, is like water soaking into sand, but, surely, only fools trust in it for refuge. Give me the Lord's name to hide in, any day. It lasts longer.

March 14th

'Better is a little with righteousness than vast revenues without justice." Proverbs 16:8

There was once a widow who had class. She was not wealthy and she lived in a drought chocked Israel. She was, in fact, down to her last meal. When asked to give that meal to a very hungry servant of God on the strength of the promise that God would supply her personal need she did not flinch from giving it away in faith. As God had promised, so He delivered. The bin of flour in her house was not used up, nor did the jar of oil run dry until the day the Lord sent rain upon a drought stricken Israel.

Up at the palace lived Queen Jezebel. Famous for her make-up and selfish conniving she had what our Proverb would call "vast revenues with injustice". No two women would have been more different and no two women ended up in starker contrast. There are few pleasures in this world to compare with the pleasures of a good conscience. The widow of Zarephath captured them.

March 15th

'Be diligent to know the state of your flocks and attend to your herds; for riches are not forever, nor does a crown endure to all generations." Proverbs 27:23-24

Recently I again visited a favourite place of mine; it is the Manchester Art Gallery where there hangs a most exquisite painting by the great painter Holman Hunt. The painting is entitled "The Hireling" and it is of a flock of sheep on a summer's afternoon under the care of a hireling shepherd who shows no diligence to know the state of his flock. The results are catastrophic.

In the painting one of the flock is in the corn; it will die of a "blown" stomach. Sheep only lie down when they feel safe and only two are lying down; they are sick. The flock are on marshy ground and will soon develop foot rot.

All this time the hireling shepherd talks to a girl about a deaths head moth be holds in his hand - a superstitious omen. The girl is so careless she has a lamb on her lap and is feeding it on sour apples. Hunt said he painted the picture in order to point out that while some pastors in the christian church were talking nonsense in their pulpits their flocks were in grave danger. Our Proverb would warn us that they still are. As the American lady said, "See that young preacher fresh out of school? He don't know my Jesus and he's an educated fool".

March 16th

'A false balance is an abomination to the Lord, but a just weight is his delight.' Proverbs 11:1

A shop assistant weighed the only chicken left in an ice-packed barrel, and announced "5 lbs". When the customer said he wanted a bigger one, the shop assistant put the chicken back in the barrel and then pulled the same chicken out. Putting it on the scales and adding pressure, the shop assistant announced, "7 lbs".

"That's fine", replied the customer, "I'll take both of them".

March 17th

"By humility and the fear of the Lord are riches and honour and life.". Proverbs 22:4

There is the joke which is told about the local church that

gave a medal to one of their leaders for his humility and then put him out of his position because he wore it! We laugh but, in truth, it is the fear of the Lord which makes a person truly humble. The happiest christians are humble christians and their humility brings them riches and honour and life.

John Ruskin put it very well when he said "I believe that the first test of a truly great person is their humility. I do not mean by humility, doubt of their own power. But really great people have a curious feeling that the greatness is not in them but through them. And they see something divine in every other person and are endlessly, foolishly, incredibly merciful".

March 18th

'The refining pot is for silver and the furnace for gold, and the man is valued by what others say of him." Proverbs 27:21

It was John Flavel who said, "Christian! Thou knowest thou carriest gun powder about thee. Desire those that carry fire to keep at a distance. It is a dangerous crisis when a proud heart meets with flattering lips".

Still, Johnny writes a better essay for his teacher next time, when he gets some praise this time. The singer sings better when someone says they have just enjoyed their last song. Even the baker bakes better bread when someone mentions that his baking is delicious. "I can live for two months on a good compliment", said Mark Twain. So can we all. Praise, though, is like a shadow; it follows the person who flies from it but flees from the person who follows it.

March 19th

'The hand of the diligent makes one rich.' Proverbs 10:4

There are people in this world, you know, who don't want

to do certain things but they are equally determined that no one else will do them! Are you tempted to stop the work you are doing in order to discuss it with such people?

We read in the Book of Nehemiah, the man who rebuilt Jerusalem's wall that he had some enemies who said to him "Come, let us meet together in one of the villages in the plain of Ono".

His answer should inspire all who want to get on with the work the Lord has called them to do despite those who would have them stop to discuss it. "I am doing a great work", wrote Nehemiah, "so that I cannot come down. Why should the work cease while I leave it to go down to you?" That's the spirit! But the verse that follows shows that he meant business; "They sent me this message four times", said Nehemiah, "and I answered them in the same manner".

Do a Nehemiah on your critics, today.

March 20th

'There is desirable treasure and oil in the dwelling of the wise but a foolish man squanders it." Proverbs 21:20

Solomon never had to use a credit card but even he might have succumbed to the subtle trap such cards bring. The debt that some folks get into because of "Instant money" through credit cards is just plain awful. I realise such cards have their uses but their dangers are surely multiple. Are you tempted to overspend with your card today? Read today's Proverb. The little card in your wallet is so flexible it can lead you to lose all your possessions in a day. Try to remember that saving beats squandering and, in the long run, "Little and often fills the purse". Sure as there's a head on your body, if your outgo exceeds your income then your upkeep will be your downfall.

"Give me neither poverty nor riches; feed me with the food you prescribe for me." Proverbs 30:8

Joni Earickenson Tada sings a beautiful song which I play on my car stereo sometimes as I drive around the city in which I live. It never fails to challenge me. In the song Joni depicts life as being like a play and everyone has a part which was written for them. She pleads in the song that she will be wise enough to play only the part that God wrote for her.

Don't you think that a whole lot of us are trying to live the part that other people have written for us? Solomon pleads that God will give him the balance in his life that will fulfil only that which God prescribes for him. The longer I live the more I am convinced that finding such a balance in your life brings the only true success. Don't you?

March 22nd

"There is one who makes himself rich, yet has nothing; and one who makes himself poor yet has great riches." Proverbs 13:7

A very daring attempt to defraud the British Branch of a Middle Eastern Bank of up to £300 million was foiled recently minutes before the money was due to be transferred.

A con man, it is said, used a facsimile machine in a north London newsagents shop and a bogus telephone line and if he had got away with it he would have carried out one of the biggest thefts yet. The plan was averted when numbers of faxes purporting to come from a London firm of Solicitors, said to have been acting for the man were found to be different from those on its letter heads! The Solicitors called in the police who called the bank which was minutes away from transferring £300 million to the man's account!

The first rule of business management is "assume nothing". Don't you think it would make a high priority rule for living too? Remember; assume nothing.

March 23rd

"The labour of the righteous leads to life, the wages of the wicked to sin.".Proverbs 10:16

So, you are discouraged. You have worked long at something and there does not seem much point in going on. How many a wife whose husband has left her, just when she needed him most, feels cheated? She has tried to put God first and raise her children with christian principles but there are those seemingly happy families who couldn't care less about anything even remotely christian all around her where no husband has walked out. Strange?

Here is a man who refuses to take bribes or cheat in his business and his business is collapsing while cheats are rolling in profits. What is it all about? It's where it's all heading is what it's all about! Note the Proverb. The labour of the righteous leads to life. The wages of the wicked leads to sin. And the wages of sin? Death. Wait and see; you'll find that right is might and purity is power, ultimately. Meantime, don't quit.

March 24th

"Getting treasures by a lying tongue is the fleeting fantasy of those who seek death." Proverbs 21:6

Poor Gehazi! Elisha's servant began so well. Note how he was the one who suggested that the Shunamite woman would love a baby. He was sensible; when he did not see her little boy raised from the dead he was not jealous that Elisha did. When the stew he organized didn't come right he didn't go off in a huff just because Elisha threw some flour in it and neutralized the poison. Notice that Elisha didn't help to make the stew nor did he go and get the flour; he simply called for both. It was Gehazi who had to do the donkey work and he served well.

Sadly he fell foul to the temptation to get-rich-quick through a lie to the Syrian army commander.

We laugh when the fable of Pinnochio says his nose grew long each time he lied. Gehazi's story, though, was no fable and what happened to him was no laugh.

God struck him with leprosy. Why? It was to make him a beacon towards everyone in order to warn them that getting treasures by a lying tongue is very serious. In fact, according to today's Proverb, it is playing with death. Selah.

March 25th

"In the house of the righteous there is much treasure but in the revenue of the wicked is trouble." Proverbs 15:6

The highest income made in any year by an individual was the gangster Al Capone's in 1927. It was reputed to have been 100 million dollars. When he died, though, how much did he leave? He left it all.

Today's Proverb is telling us that those who know and trust the Lord may not necessarily have much money but that does not mean they are treasureless. They have Christ and he is the greatest treasure of all.

Recently I came upon a little piece called "The Innkeeper's Lament".

Think about it.

"All my patrons now are dead,
And forgotten, but today
All the world to peace is led
By the ones I sent away.
It was my unlucky fate
To be born that inn to own
Against Christ I shut my gate
Oh, if only I had known!"

March 26th

"Honour the Lord from your wealth." Proverbs 3:9-10

What happens if you have virtually no money to give? Does it mean that you are not wealthy and cannot, therefore, honour the Lord from your wealth? No. You can speak, can't you? There is nothing as pleasant as a cheerful word of greeting. You can smile, can't you? It takes 72 muscles to frown and only 14 to smile. So, smile, friend, smile! You can be considerate with the feelings of others, can't you? As the man said, there are three sides to a controversy; yours, mine and the right one! You can do a kind act somewhere throughout today, can't you? Wash dishes, run an errand? Visit someone who needs cheering?

Try to learn people's names. More than money, more than position, more than virtually anything people appreciate other people calling them by name. Don't get into the journalistic practice of just using a surname; use a person's christian name where appropriate. It is a decent christian practice. You would be surprised how folks appreciate it.

See? You are wealthier than you thought, aren't you? Honour the Lord with your wealth.

"I wisdom ... traverse the way of the righteous ... that I may cause those who love me to inherit wealth." Proverbs 8:20-21

"I've seen all of them", said Carol Frazer, an Elvis Presley fan. "Love Me Tender", 107 times, "Loving You", 110 times, "King Creole", 91 times, and "Jailhouse Rock", 79 times. She said she had 40,000 pictures of him.

Carol was only one of the millions of Elvis Presley fans who according to the writer Katrika Matson was the highest paid performer in history. The price he paid in terms of his emotional and physical health was incalculable. He took a lot of pills to keep going and a careful analysis of his blood revealed that 10 different drugs were present in the singer's bloodstream when he died. There interaction had caused his heart to fail.

I can never forget speaking at a Convention, once, where Elvis's stepbrother gave his christian testimony. He told how, a few days before Elvis died that one of his entourage told him that this girl kept ringing him up tell him that he should be living for Jesus. "It's high time we were all living for Jesus", replied Elvis. Was he beginning to fully realise where true wealth lay? Are you?

March 28th

"A good man leaves an inheritance to his children's children."
Proverbs 13:22

What endures? "I believe that life is a mess ... it is like yeast, a ferment, a thing that moves and may move for a month, an hour, a year, or a hundred years, but that in the end will cease to move ... the lucky eat the most and move the longest, that is all", wrote Jack London, the world's first millionaire novelist.

No, Jack, no. As a child I read "Call of the Wild", your brilliant book which sold a million copies at the time it was published. You had great gift, Jack, but you were wrong about life. Life handed into the hands of the Lord Jesus is no mess, does not run on luck and its eternal quality does not cease to move.

"This is eternal life, that they may know you, the only true God, and Jesus Christ whom you sent", said Christ. Let's live our lives for Him and we will never regret it. What's more, we will, by doing this leave an inheritance to your children's children that money could never buy. Believe me.

March 29th

"He who restrains his lips is wise. The tongue of the righteous is choice silver." Proverbs 10:19-20

Did you know that in order for a bee to sting, 22 muscles are brought into action?

It involves 23 separate sets of movements in the sting mechanism among them, the outward thrust of the stinging shaft, the depression of the shaft, and the movements of the lancets on the stylet of the sting.

It is all highly complicated, yet we are informed that the complicated mechanism does not call for any particular skill on the part of the bee, the stinging being largely an automatic act.

Speaking a word is also a highly complicated mechanism as far as the body is concerned, but, you don't need to have much skill in speaking in order to sting folks with your words.

This little poem was put into my hand the other day and I pass it on to you;

"A Word"
A careless word may kindle strife
A cruel word may wreck a life
A bitter word may hate instil
A brutal word may smite and kill
A gracious word may light a day
A timely word may lessen stress
A loving word may heal and bless.

March 30th

"The wealth of the sinner is stored up for the righteous."
Proverbs 13:22

$1 \times 9 + 2 = 11$
$12 \times 9 + 3 = 111$
$123 \times 9 + 4 = 1111$
$1234 \times 9 + 5 = 11111$
$12345 \times 9 + 6 = 111111$
$123456 \times 9 + 7 = 1111111$
$1234567 \times 9 + 8 = 11111111$
$12345678 \times 9 + 9 = 111111111$
$123456789 \times 9 + 10 = 1111111111$

It seems incredible, doesn't it? So does today's Proverb. When you think of it, though, the spoils of Egypt became Israel's, Laban's wealth became Jacob's, Hamman's wealth became Mordecai and Esther's. God, according to Ecclesiastes 2:26, gives to the sinner "the work of gathering and collecting that he may give to him who is good before God".

Hitler's radio station in Monte Carlo, built for Nazi propaganda is now the headquarters for Trans World Radio's Gospel broadcast to Europe! So, don't get jealous of the prosperity of evil men; before they are finished you would be surprised where their wealth will end up.

"Happy is the man who finds wisdom, and the man who gains understanding; for her proceeds are better than the profits of silver, and her gain than fine gold. She is more precious than rubies, and all the things you may desire cannot compare with her. Length of days is in her right hand, in her left hand riches and honour."
Proverbs 3:13-16

We have, during this month, studied the views of the Book of Proverbs on the subject of wealth. I'd like to finish our studies with a little comment from the very famous marketing and management entrepreneur called Mark McCormack. Mr. McCormack's corporation represents such major and diverse events as Wimbledon and the Nobel Foundation. I was intrigued to read that when a famous sports personality signed up with him he said he could make him only two guarantees. One, if he didn't know something he would tell him and second, that when he didn't know something he would find someone who did. Now, that's wisdom.

We too, as we have studied this subject together, have discovered how small our knowledge is and how tiny our wisdom. Yet, that wisdom is freely available from God. All we have to do is ask him. If we don't know something we can go to the one who has the key to all knowledge and talk to him about it. Let's talk to him often and may we always remember until our very last breath that the fear of the Lord is the beginningof wisdom.

$\mathcal{A}$PRIL

APRIL

We have all been caught by April Fool pranks. I know of an entire school which was brought out on a fire drill and lined out in their appropriate places. There was a special marked out spot for the Headmistress and when she eventually stepped into it she was informed that she was an April Fool. Nasty?

It will be even nastier for us, if, in life, we deliberately follow the way of fools. Their way of life is very cryptically highlighted in the Book of Proverbs. With verve and warning Solomon seeks to show us the folly of fools but also balances his teaching with the wisdom of the wise. We shall look at both as we move through this month of blossoming Spring.

April 1st

"Understanding is a well-spring of life to him who has it. But the correction of fools is folly." Proverbs 16:22

Discipline. Who likes it? It can come from God's hand in a thousand different ways and if it is heeded we are much the better for it. Consider the opal. It is made only of the desert dust, sand and silica and owes its beauty and preciousness to a defect. It is a stone with a broken heart. It is full of minute fissures which admit air and the air reflects the light. That's the source of its lovely hues.

We are too well aware of the cracks and dust in our lives, but, God allows all kinds of discipline to come and so, through it all, He makes His opal. If we yield to His disciplining hand we can give back the lovely hues of His light. Fools, of course, wouldn't even recognise God's discipline if they saw it. No lovely hues emit from their empty lives. So, don't be a fool, heed the sign which says "yield".

"Let a man meet a bear robbed of her cubs, rather than a fool in his folly." Proverbs 17:12

This Proverb is saying that animals are sometimes easier to deal with than people.

To meet a bear robbed of her cubs is far less dangerous than to meet a fool in his folly.

Are you bent on some foolish and stupid errand at the moment? All the reproof, reason and kind pleadings of your friends cannot get you to see the folly of what you are doing. People can escape from an enraged bear, but, the folk in your family and its circle cannot escape from you. You know in your own heart that you are wrong but folly is blinkered.

Think about today's Proverb. Let shame unblinker you. Did not David swear that he would kill every male in Nabal's house? He soon discovered that one of his greatest supporters lived there! David was persuaded to put aside his folly. Follow his example. Let your enemy go. Go on serving the Lord and when your ways please Him even your enemies will be at peace with you.

"Like a flitting sparrow, like a flying swallow, so a curse without cause shall not alight." Proverbs 26:2

Stand by a river one day and watch the swallows as they dive over the surface of the water. One of their dives may come toward you and it may even cause you to lift your hand to protect yourself. I know. I've done it. But the swallow will not fly into you. It will soar, even at the last moment, over your head. Even the little sparrow itself will flit past you.

So it is with many of the things in life that worry you. They never come. The thing you thought would wreck you never even had a foundation. It is true, though, that groundless fears can be a real menace.

Don't be foolish and spend your life worrying about the things that will never happen. Why be a fool and waste your energy on nothing?

April 4th

"Do you see a man who is wise in his own eyes? There is more hope of a fool than for him." Proverbs 26:12

God singles this person out. He wants to nail his folly. He chooses language which for ever encapsulates the stupidity of his action. This person leans on a broken bridge and will soon be in the water. What's wrong? He is conceited. He thinks he is wise.

Someone has defined a conceited person as being one who, on his birthday, sends his parents a telegram of congratulations! Now let's not get carried away; you can deliberately choose to act wisely and know when you are doing so.

It's when people think they are acting wisely and put it down to themselves as being the source of their actions that brings them into the category of the conceited. Anyone acting according to God's word is very wise but they know where they get their wisdom.

In Austria recently the top medal winning medical graduate in the nation, when being presented with his award by the President of Austria publicly acknowledged that Jesus Christ in His life was the source of his success. His parents had threatened to cut him off if he would acknowledge Christ. He went ahead anyway and the great gathering of academics and leaders of Austria gave him an ovation!

Never be ashamed, christian, of the source of your blessing. Never. Acknowledge it to someone today.

April 5th

"The fear of the Lord is the beginning of knowledge, but fools despise wisdom and instruction.' Proverbs 1:7

I was at a public function recently and "grace" was offered at the beginning of the meal. Afterwards a leader in our community objected. Church and state were separate, he said, and what on earth were we doing giving thanks to God at a public function that had nothing to do with spiritual things? The answer has to do with the fear of the Lord. To acknowledge God in public brings a tempering to mankind's love of cleverness. Have you noticed on television that, in our 'three minute' culture, the ads are so clever we sometimes forget that all we admire is their cleverness. Cleverness is all. Such a thing is dangerous in any culture.

As Alan Ackborne, one of Britain's leading playwrights has said, "All great art comes from people who recognise that there is something higher than themselves". In my life I call that the fear of the Lord. Don't you? It is an affectionate reverence for God in public and private life. Only fools despise it.

April 6th

"The heart of him who has understanding seeks knowledge, but the mouth of fools feeds on foolishness."
Proverbs 15:14

If you want to know how educated people are just get them off the subject they specialise in! Some of the most brilliant people in the world couldn't even fry an egg. Humility about the limitations of our knowledge is the stepping stone to greater knowledge. Remember that every person you meet is better at something than you are.

Most fools, though, never learn. They have no enthusiasm for wisdom or knowledge and when they get together their conversation is just full of foolishness. Foolishness is their food and drink. Make up your mind to avoid them. Be like David. What did he say? He said "You, through your commandments make me wiser than my enemies; for they are ever with me. I have more understanding than all my teachers for your testimonies are my meditation. I understand more than the ancients because I keep your precepts. I have restrained my feet from every evil way that I may keep your word". Now that's what I call really living. What do you think?

April 7th

"A desire accomplished is sweet to the soul but it is an abomination to fools to depart from evil." Proverbs 13:19

Does time seem long for you? Are your trials heavy? Is your confidence failing? You have desired for something but have not found it; perhaps, if you had, it would not have been good for you. It may be a mercy that you didn't get what you asked for. I know if I had got all I longed for I would have sadly missed the wonderful things God has given me which are infinitely better.

What is good will be granted. If you delight yourself in the Lord he will give you the desires of your heart. Why? Because if you are delighting yourself in Him you will desire only what He desires and that can only be good, and, very sweet. Fools don't want such sweetness. They love what

God hates. So, as you move through the day, delight yourself in the Lord and wait for your desires to be accomplished. You will not be disappointed.

April 8th

"Why is there in the hand of a fool the purchase price of wisdom, since he has no heart for it?" Proverbs 17:16

Consider the Japanese. Did you know that it takes the average Japanese wage earner thirteen years to save enough for a down payment on a two bed apartment in Tokyo costing roughly around £250,000? Did you know that the total value of Tokyo's land is worth more than the entire United States?

At the other extreme, there are people in India who are so poor that they live under hedges or on the street.

Are you, in your circumstances, not greatly advantaged? What today's Proverb is after is to challenge you with the advantages that lie at your hand.

If I have a fear in my life it is the fear of having an opportunity given to me by God and missing it by frittering away my time on something frivolous. Fools have no heart to take advantage of their advantages.

Let us take note of the fact that 'if you will not when you may: you may not when you will.'

April 9th

"A foolish son is a grief to his father and bitterness to her who bore him." Proverbs 17:25

This Proverb has been experienced by millions of people. Eve knew all about it and so did David. What shall we say of Samson's parents? The litany is endless. But it can be reversed.

Every day, somewhere in the world the back door latch is lifted and a prodigal comes home. Few words are said but an awful lot of hugging goes on! The years of bitterness, of anxiety and grief are over. The words "I'm sorry" are enough. The rancour turns to laughter, the murky rebellion turns to music. I tell you, it happens every day.

So, Prodigal, go home and Parent, keep trusting. Today just might be the day.

April 10th

'Do not speak in the hearing of a fool, for he will despise the wisdom of your words". Proverbs 23:9

You wouldn't give pearls to pigs, would you? You are very foolish if you tell the precious things of your life to fools. It is even heart wrenching to see children never to speak of adults telling what is personally precious to them in the hearing of those who despise it.

Little children can be excused but what excuse is there for you if you know there are fools in your company and you spill out the treasures of your heart for their big feet to walk all over? There is a time to keep silence and a time to speak. The presence of fools will particularly help you to know when to keep silent. Selah.

April 11th

"A wise man fears and departs from evil but a fool rages and is self confident." Proverbs 14:16

Caution is not a bad characteristic. The wise person fears the Lord and is therefore cautious when faced with decisions. The very appearance of evil is something to be shunned. It may mean being called "too shy", "too diffedent", "too indecisive", "spineless", but, better to be criticised for holding back than to be ruined by plunging forward.

Men and women who go too far too fast cause violence to erupt. Fools who are arrogant and careless ride rough shod over circumstances, history and sensitivities and it often ends, not only with heartache, but, bloodshed. Let me plead caution as you go about your business today. Watch it! Too far East is West.

April 12th

"O you simple ones, understand prudence, and you fools be of an understanding heart. Listen, for I will speak of excellent things and from the opening of my lips will come right things; for my mouth will speak truth." Wisdom speaking in Proverbs 8:5-6

Ivana Trump the New York socialite, at the time of writing, is alleged by her friends to need $4 million a year to keep her in the style to which she is accustomed. Her minimum budget needs were compiled by socialite watchers at Woman's World Daily, which chronicles the lifestyles of the rich and famous. They break it down to the following. They say it will cost her at least $1,875,000 for a suitable apartment in New York. She will then need $1,562,000 for a Long Island beach house. She will need $150,000 for gowns alone to stay in the mainstream of America's high society. She will need $125,000 for entertainment and another $16,250 for flowers. Her lunches with girlfriends will cost her $8,125, although she will not be eating out every day. She can expect to spend $31,000 on interior designs and her hairdresser will cost her $15,000. Regular manicures will come to $1,950. She will spend $40,000 on a nanny for her children and $9,000 for her own personal aerobic trainer. A further $60,000 will be earmarked for "miscellaneous needs".

The experts say their estimates are by no means extravagant or outrageous.

Speaking of money Sir John Paul Getty is reckoned to earn $3 a second and is now estimated to be worth $1,200 million. He said recently "Money doesn't bring automatic happiness. There have been many times when I have cursed it".

The divorced heiress the Honourable Mrs. Charlotte Morrison whose wealth has been assessed at £55 million spoke recently of finding it difficult being alone, "Sometimes I think Oh I'd love to talk to somebody or I wish there was somebody here".

Through all of this we hear the word of Wisdom, who is Christ Himself, crying to us that a person's life "Does not consist in the abundance of the things which they possess". Heed him.

April 13th

"Do not reprove a scoffer, lest he hate you; rebuke a wise man, and he will love you. Give instruction to a wise man, and he will be still wiser." Proverbs 9:8-9

It is a great temptation to reprove scoffers. It doesn't win them, though. They will often hate you as a result. The best way to deal with scoffers is to go on, going on with what is right. Someone once publicly attacked a man called Dr. Fuller. "God bless him", said Dr. Fuller when he heard of it. "You don't seem too upset, Doctor", said his informant. "Why should I let someone else decide how I am going to act?", replied Fuller.

Rebuke wise people and they will love you. Give instruction to wise people and they will be still wiser. It seems to me that a wise person listening even to a fool will learn more than a fool listening to a wise person. Even from the errors of others wise people correct their own. So, make a few corrections today.

April 14th

"Incline your ear and hear the words of the wise, and apply your heart to my knowledge; for it is a pleasant thing if you keep them within you; let them all be fixed upon your lips."
Proverbs 22:17-18

Do you ever listen to a wise person? Keep a notebook handy. Store up what they say and keep it for an occasion when it will be useful. That is what this Proverb says.

I was only a lad and I remember going to hear Dr. Martyn Lloyd-Jones preach in Belfast. About 3,000 people turned up to hear what he had to say about the current state of the church. I remember him turning to his audience and saying a sentence which has burned in me for at least two decades. "Why?" he said, "Is Christ not enough for you, any more?"

Why not say something to someone today that would be worth their while storing away in their mind? After all, as Plato said, "Wise men talk because they have something to say; fools, because they have to say something".

April 15th

"The way of life winds upward for the wise, that he may turn away from hell below." Proverbs 15:24

Everything in this life eventually disintegrates. See that lovely new car? The breakers yard will hear it crunch to pieces one day. See that massive tree? Wind and disease will soon have it. See that attractive home? Paint will peel, doors will stick, drains will clog. Even the best fitting clothes will have to be replaced.

But see the people who are wise? Their way of life does not go down. This very day I visited an old woman in a former Scottish mining village before sitting down to write this piece. She was very ill but on speaking with her about spiritual things her face brightened and she told me how she was anticipating meeting the Saviour; "He is the only comfort I have", she has just told me. How different to the words of Scott Fitzgerald lying near death. The great writer was an alcoholic. "What", he wrote "if this were the night that prefigures the night after death? Only the endless repetition of the sordid and semi-tragic. No road, no hope". I'll take the old lady's truth any day. Won't you?

April 16th

"In the multitude of words sin is not lacking, but he who restrains his lips is wise." Proverbs 10:19

According to Levy in "The Adaptive Advantages of Cerebral Asymmetry and Communnication" in the Annals of the New York Academy of Sciences (Volume 229:264-72 - Thought I'd better let you know my source!) the average man speaks roughly 12,500 words a day. In contrast the average woman speaks more than 25,000!

Researchers have found that even in a hospital nursery girls have more lip movement than boys. Women, of course, are more intuitive, can do more fine detail work and have more imagination than men. Men are more analytical, factual, and given to "black and white" thinking.

Despite the differences all of us could do with a button on our lip. Even light words weigh heavy in God's balance. Button up on your lip today and you will avoid a lot of transgression.

"There are four things which are little on the earth, but they are exceedingly wise; the ants are a people not strong, yet they prepare their food in the summer." Proverbs 30:24-25

The ant is considered wise because of its dedication to the principle of preparation. Are you? The Proverb tells us that ants are weak. In fact, you could crush a thousand with your foot, but, their weakness does not stop their diligence to prepare in summer for winter. As the song says of the ants diligence in a rubber tree plantation, "Oops! There goes another rubber tree plant!"

Recently I sat in the presence of a Lord of the Realm who was speaking publicly on a burning issue. Unfortunately he had a "mental blank" right in the middle of his speech. I felt heart sorry for him as his face turned grey. A little preparation on a written script would have made all the difference. Churchill, you know, never really made a spontaneous speech in his life. A valet once rushed to Churchill's bath thinking he was being summoned. "No", said the great orator, "I was not addressing you, I was addressing the House of Commons". Ant work, eh? Don't you think faith breeds organization?

"The rock badgers are a feeble folk, yet they make their homes in the crags." Proverbs 30:26

Consider the coney. Known as the "rock badger" they look like a short legged and short eared rabbit without a tail. They are rock dwellers and are very, very timid. The Proverb would remind us that what the coneys lack in strength they make up in wisdom. They make sure that they make their houses in the holes of inaccessible rocks. The coney is no fool!

Let's take a leaf from the coney's book. Let's be like the little girl who was asked what she did when Satan knocked upon the door of her life; "I send Jesus to answer the door!", she replied. He is my hiding place. Is he yours?

April 19th

"The locusts have no king, yet they all advance in ranks."
Proverbs 30:2

"When the swarms of locusts came", wrote Jerome, "and filled the lower regions of the air they flew in such order, by the divine appointment, and kept their place as exactly as when several piles or partly coloured stones are carefully placed in a pavement so as not to be a hairs-breadth out of their several ranks".

Pity we didn't have their wisdom, isn't it? The christian church has a king but looking at it one would sometimes wonder if they ever listen to him. The division between christians is often frightening. Try, as you go through this day, to strive for "the unity of the spirit in the bond of peace". How? Follow the King and he will tell you in what rank you ought to serve. When he does, stick to it.

April 20th

"The spider skilfully grasps with its hands, and it is in kings'
palaces." Proverbs 30:28

Have you not stood on a dewy morning and marvelled at the precise, mathematical exactness of a spider's web as it glints in the sun? You'll find the spider's work displayed, even in kings' palaces.

And you? What work has God given you to do? Stay at it with diligence. Prepare for your Sunday school class as if you were going to speak to a 100,000 people. One of your class may one day speak of Christ to 100,000 people. Raise that family of yours for the Lord and they in turn might raise theirs for the same purpose. Writing a letter? It might be the last one you will write; make it worth reading. Making a phone call? Guard your lips. The walls have ears. Don't be too proud to learn from the little insects we have studied over the past few days. Give yourself to the work God has called you to with diligence and He will give you the wisdom you need. And remember; if these insects would teach us one thing they would teach us that big is not necessarily great.

April 21st

"A wise man scales the city of the mighty, and brings down the trusted stronghold." Proverbs 21:22

She was incensed. The treatment of black people by white people in America's "Deep South" was abominable. Women had little to say in her society, so, she lifted the only weapon she could find; her pen. She declared war on slavery with a story which so opened the eyes of whites to what they were doing to blacks it led to the abolition of slavery in the United States. Her name? Harriet Beecher Stowe. Her book? "Uncle Tom's Cabin".

In England a man, small of stature but great of heart called William Wilberforce, a member of Parliament who was a committed christian, stood bravely and argued for the abolition of the slave trade in the British Empire. He looked so weak and failed so often to achieve his goal. Yet, finally, he saw his dream fulfilled and an Act was passed through the British House of Commons putting away the curse of slavery.

One used his tongue and influence and the other used her pen but both, in God's hand, scaled what seemed and impossible height and won through. Both knew the Lord and did what they could. How about you? Try scaling a few strongholds with wisdom this week. There is no telling what might happen.

April 22nd

"Scorners ensnare a city, but wise men turn away wrath."
Proverbs 29:8

"There was a little city with few men in it", says the Book of Ecclesiastes, "and a great man came against it, besieged it, and built great snares around it. Now there was found in it a poor wise man, and he by his wisdom delivered the city. Yet no one remembered that same poor man". I often wonder who the man was and how lonely he felt. Has someone in your life, saved you from a terrible mistake? It may be years since you have contacted him. Has a teacher, years ago, been a help in steering you in the right direction in your life? When did you ever drop him or her a line to say thank you? People who are wise seldom get any praise for their application of wisdom. Why not remember such people in your life and contact them this month? You would be amazed how they are forgotten.

April 23rd

"The father of the righteous will greatly rejoice, and he who begets a wise child will delight in him.".Proverbs 23:24

It was Paul Tournier who said "Many parents are extremely authoritarian and many parents are extremely permissive.

95

Most parents are in between those extremes. But whether parents are extremely authoritarian or extremely permissive or somewhere in between, if their children turn out alright, it's by the grace of God".

Paul Tournier was right. Yet, the availability of the grace of God does not take away from the responsibility of fathers to be role-models for their children. That means more than telling them the Gospel story. Children want a father they can respect. They want a father who loves their mother with all his heart. They want a father who is big enough to laugh at himself. They don't want a big moan sitting in the chair. They want a father who when he says "No" means "No" and when he says "Yes" he means "Yes". So, fathers let's get busy.

April 24th

"A wise man is strong, yes, a man of knowledge increases strength.". Proverbs 24:5

If you doubt that knowledge is power just check out the life of Albert Einstein. Einstein was probably one of the greatest scientific thinkers of all time and he showed that mass was a form of energy and realised if the whole of a carbon atom could be turned into useable energy about 3 million times as much energy would be released as when the carbon combined with oxygen atoms to burn his coal!

It had long been known that the amount of energy in a moving object depended on the weight of the object multiplied by the square of its speed. Einstein's theory was that the amount of energy actually "locked up" in a substance depends on the weight of the substance multiplied by the square of the speed of light. If you doubt him just check out the proof of it in, for example, an atomic power station where huge amounts of power are produced from small lumps of uranium.

Knowledge is power but consider the power of spiritual knowledge. It was Daniel who pointed out that "the people who know their God shall be strong and carry out great exploits". Spiritual knowledge leads to changed lives. Now that is power that a scientist by his thinking could never produce. It is the best kind of power.

April 25th

"The ear that hears the reproof of life will abide among the wise."
Proverbs 15:31

I remember the day she warned me. I had begun to "take things for granted" and was beginning to forget all of God's great benefits toward me. She was courageous but her warning caught me amid ships. I turned back to my work, humbled and yet, somehow, encouraged.Such friends are few but if you listen to them the benefits are incalculable.

Have you heard about the two grasshoppers who jumped into a pail of milk? One groaned and moaned and sank to the bottom. The other remained cheerful, kicking his legs, churning until the milk became butter. That grasshopper then walked over the top and jumped away. If we cultivate a contented attitude in our troubles they will become stepping stones to happiness. I had been warned and joined the "escaped" grasshopper. I still need reminding, though. Don't you?

April 26th

"A good name is to be chosen rather than great riches. Loving favour rather than silver and gold." *Proverbs 22:1*

"The Times" of March 8th 1990 carried a headline that

drove me back to the Proverbs. It read "Win a store lose a name". It concerned the Fayad brothers who, in a government report were accused of lying repeatedly about their family background, their early business life and their wealth.

It is said that in 1985 the Fayad brothers used £615 million in their bid for the most famous department store in Britain, Harrods. They won a store but they have now lost a name.

Which is better? Which is wiser? To lie and gain in the immediate or tell the truth and gain in the long run? The answer must be obvious but many fools choose to lie. People lie with half-truths, with double meanings, with flattery, and with exaggeration every day in order to gain money and position. They forget that loving favour and a good name are not marketable. They are earned.

April 27th

"How much better it is to get wisdom than gold! And to get understanding is to be chosen rather than silver." Proverbs 16:16

Here is a man or woman and they have all the possessions a heart could wish, yet, they cannot understand why they can't handle life. Surely we must be reminded of the fact that it is one thing to have money and it is another thing to have the wisdom how to handle it. It is one thing to have academic prowess but it is entirely another thing to have the wisdom to apply knowledge.

I love what Charles Bridges says when he comments "Calculate in the balances of the santuary the overwhelming interests of heaven above earth, of the soul above the body, of eternity above time; and who will dispute this verdict? Multitudes labour night and day for gold; yet miss the treasure. But who was ever disappointed in the effort to get wisdom? When has earnestness and prayer failed of success?"

In our Lord Jesus Christ are hidden "all the treasures of wisdom and knowledge" (Colossians 2:3). Look to Him in prayer today and ask Him for wisdom and understanding in how to use your possessions wisely and in how to apply your knowledge humbly and to lasting effect. He will not fail to help you; He's only a prayer away. Ask Him.

April 28th

"The rod and reprof give wisdom but a child left to himself brings shame to his mother." Proverbs 29:15

It has been said that there are two kinds of discipline, spanking and consequential discipline. As for the first I heard of a man who said his father belonged to a denomination which believed in the "laying on of hands" and that he sure laid them on!

According to Scripture those who spare the rod hate their children (Proverbs 13:24). I like what Larry Christenson says. He points out that "There's only one place for a spanking - on the back end. You should never cuff, hit or abuse a child. Biblical discipline is the antithesis of child abuse. God created the rear end with lots of padding and nerve endings - a perfect combination for discipline".

Consequential discipline is also important. If you let your children do something within limitations and they override your limitations, then the consequence is that next time they ask the answer will be a definite "No".

Fail to apply either of these disciplines and our Proverb warns that wisdom will not be an attribute of your child and shame will be brought into the family.

May God give us as parents grace to apply these things for they are easier said than done.

April 29th

"A man who isolates himself seeks his own desire; he rages against all wise judgement." Proverbs 18:1

The Israelites headed for the rocks and caves for eight successive years because of the nomadic raids at harvest time by the Midianites. It was a pathetic sight. Everybody did that which was right in their own eyes. They isolated themselves.

The problem was still there, though, and only one man had the secret of defeating the enemy. His name was Gideon and he kept the food supply going. He threshed his wheat and hid it from the Midianites. No wonder the angel said "The Lord is with you, you mighty man of valour".

Is there someone reading this book today and you are hidding in TV soap operas, or novels, or a weekend hideaway and have long since given up going to hear God's Word preached amongst His people? You might rage in your heart against your circumstances that have driven you to isolation but you know that away down deep you are very hungry for spiritual food. You won't get it in isolationism. Come on, get back to God's Word and the fellowship of His people. No matter what circumstance comes against us in any year we must keep the food supply going. It is there for the taking.

April 30th

"Buy the truth, and do not sell it, also wisdom and instruction and understanding." Proverbs 23:23

We began the month together studying Proverbs regarding

fools but gradually, through its days we have moved to the Proverbs which highlight the wise and their wisdom. Here we come, as April stands back for May, to Solomon's great warning that we must not exchange wisdom for trifles.

Esau sold wisdom for a plate of lentil soup. Saul sold the truth to please his men. Absalom sold it for vanity. Gehazi sold it for some designer clothes. Gideon sold it for a jewel bedecked apron. Herod sold it for political clout. The young ruler sold it for his possession. Demas sold it for "this present age". Few in this world heed Christ's call to "Buy from me gold refined in the fire, that you may be rich". Such gold cannot be bought with money but it will cost you your life. Choose it and live.

May

"My anger", said the lady, "is over in a minute". "So is a shot from a gun", came the reply. Too true.

This month I want to speak not in anger but of the Proverbs that deal with the subject of anger. It is a very practical subject and I want to balance it with those beautiful Proverbs that speak of kindness. Perhaps what could have been stormy days this month, because of your anger, will be turned into calm days because of your kindness. The Lord can help you make the difference, if you let Him.

May 1st

"For jealousy is a husband's fury; therefore he will not spare in the day of vengeance." Proverbs 6:34

She sat before me and told me the sad, sordid story of her unfaithfulness to her husband. The havoc she brought on her quality of life was pitiful to see.

There are some forms of jealousy justifiable and jealousy within marriage is one of them. If a man or woman is not jealous when their partner is unfaithful there would be something very wrong with their marriage. So it is with God; when His bride, which is the church, flirts with other gods the scripture teaches that it provokes Him to jealousy and he will move to protect his relationship with his bride. He will chastise his people. If he didn't there would be something very wrong with his relationship with his people. Are you flirting?

May 2nd

"He who is quick tempered acts foolishly." Proverbs 14:17

Kruschev banged his shoe on the desk of the U.N. and promised to bury us. Glasnost and Peristroika were not "in" words at the time! Then there was that famous Mary Decker reaction to Zola Budd. Remember that? The problem is that kind of thing is what people remember, because, life is 10% what happens to you and 90% how you react to it.

I know of one man who bought a new table for his wife for Christmas. She turned up her nose at it and he got so mad he took the table to the bottom of the garden, took a hatchet to it and chopped it to pieces. My wife always says that she wishes she had got to him before he got to the bottom of the garden because she would gladly have relieved him of his table!

Watch quick temper today because it can make you do a thing that will be the only thing people will remember you for.

May 3rd

"He who is slow to wrath has great understanding."
Proverbs 14:29

Many of us live on the brink of irritation because we are caught up in the fast pace of this world. Our overloaded schedules get us into a pace of life which gets us into the habit of only hearing half of what the other person is saying before we respond.

Recently a plot to get triggers for nuclear bombs through Britain to Iraq was discovered. We are informed that it is easy to make a nuclear bomb, it is the triggers that are hard to get. It is not so with many folks' tongues; a little pressure on the trigger of the half-cocked pistol of their tongues is enough to blow marriages, churches, offices, schools, you name it, apart. The slow-too-wrath person is a gem; are you one?

"A harsh word stirs up anger." Proverbs 15:1

Think of the harsh words people use to discourage so many. "You nit-wit", and, an honest effort is blasted. "It's her own fault", and, in anger her recovery is set back, years. "He's immature", and, he quits trying. "Now if I were you I'd leave right now", and, in anger, he does and makes the biggest mistake of his life.

If you use harsh words have you any idea of what you are stirring? Have you stopped to think where it will end? They will come back to you to haunt you, like they did to Saul who so berated David. "I have played the fool", he admitted, "and have erred exceedingly". It ended in his suicide, not David's. Harsh words will do more harm to you than they ever will to your enemy. Let sleeping unrighteous wrath lie. Don't stir him or he will rip you apart.

May 5th

"A wrathful man stirs up strife but he who is slow to anger allays contention." Proverbs 15:18

Pride has a way of making even the smallest offences appear as unforgivable holocausts, but, the plain fact remains that if you take the humble place and don't quarrel there won't be one. Quarrels depend on people far more than the thing quarrelled over.

So, you want to be a peacemaker? Carry about with you an atmosphere in which quarrels die a natural death. Ask God to give you that personal atmosphere. Few there are who have an allaying-contention-ministry. You could be one of those precious few.

"If you have been foolish and exalting yourself, or if you have devised evil, put your hand on your mouth. For as the churning of milk produces butter, and as wringing the nose produces blood, so the forcing of wrath produces strife." Proverbs 30:32-33

My aunt Lily was a tremendous maker of butter; I can hear her using the churn, yet, when I was a little child on the farm at Aughlisnafin in Co. Down. Back and forward the milk would churn until eventually golden butter would be produced. It will not be anything golden you produce, if, after you have done something foolish or something downright sinful you protest innocence or mouth platitudes of false repentance. Our Proverb is warning us that when we have erred the best thing to do is to keep quiet. When we are wrong let's admit it and say no more. If we keep talking about the matter we will only churn wrath and produce strife. The least said the least mended. Selah.

"He who is slow to anger is better than the mighty, and he who rules his spirit than he who takes his city." Proverbs 16:32

It is important to establish that anger is a God given emotion. We must never think that it is an unwanted emotional appendage that good christians learn to cut off. Paul clearly taught that christians are to "be angry". Righteous anger should be every bit a part of the christian's life as it is an attribute of the God they worship. But when Paul says "Be angry" he adds "Be angry and sin not; let not the sun go down on your wrath". That doesn't mean "Be angry until sunset" because then our wrath might lengthen with the days and christians in Greenland would have plenty of scope for wrath because their days last beyond a quarter of the year! No. Paul is warning us not to nurse resentment. He is saying don't go to bed with unrighteous anger.

So, there is such a thing as righteous anger but we had better keep it under control. Ask God's Spirit to help you to rule your spirit today and you will be mightier than one who takes a city. Try to remember that anyone who causes you to lose your self-control, conquers you.

May 8th

"The discretion of the man makes him slow to anger and it is to his glory to overlook a transgression.".Proverbs 19:11

"You can afford to be magnimonious, Derick", said a friend when I spoke to him of being aggrieved over something. Somehow that little phrase has stuck in my mind for years; "You can afford to be magnimonious ... you can afford to be magnimonious."

When you think about it, for a christian not to be magnimonious would be a contradiction in terms. Were we not shown great mercy at Calvary? Who of us deserved such kindness? The God whose wrath was raised against our sin devised a means whereby he himself, in the person of Christ, bore his own wrath against our sins. The thing is just too wonderful to measure. If you boil with resentment against someone, show mercy and pity where possible. It is a beautiful thing to do. Don't let the brightness of your idealism blind your compassion.

At the risk of being repetitious let me repeat the words of my friend once more; "You can afford to be magnimonious". Be tough but tender.

"A man of great wrath will suffer punishment; for if you deliver him you will have to do it again." Proverbs 19:19

All through life you will hear people describe someone as "She's her own worst enemy" or "If only he'd realise it he's beating himself with a stick". I watched a child, one day, in a fit of temper actually beat itself!

Unjustified anger coming over and over again in bouts of ungovernable temper in your life will land you in fresh trouble time and time again. Cool it, friend, cool it. If you do people might even begin to like you! You can't always be hitting the ceiling without making people think there's something wrong upstairs.

"A gift in secret pacifies anger and a bribe behind the back, strong wrath." Proverbs 21:14

A gift, yes, but a bribe, no. Let us never be guilty of bribing people. When it came to dealing with God's anger against sin the Israelites were allowed to offer a minchah, a gift. It could, with regard to the grain offering, be in three forms (see Leviticus 2); fine flour, cakes baked, fried or grilled, or the green heads of grain which came up fifty days before harvesting.

The first spoke of Christ's precious body, the second of that body broken and the third of the resurrection which came fifty days before the harvest the Holy Spirit brought at Pentecost. What a gift God gave when he gave us the Lord Jesus and no gift appeased his wrath like it before or since, or ever will. There was no bribery in it.

A thoughtful gift to pacify someones anger might not come amiss today. But be careful for with human beings the boundary between a gift and a bribe is exceedingly thin. According to Ecclesiastes 7:7 "A bribe debases the heart". You would never want to be guilty of doing that, would you? So, avoid bribes like the plague.

May 11th

"Make no friendship with an angry man and with a furious man do not go, lest you learn his ways and set a snare for your own soul." Proverbs 22:24

To fall into a snare that someone else has set for you is bad enough but to fall into one that you have set for yourself is terrible. Our Proverb tells us plainly that if we make friendship with a person given to downright bad temper we are setting a snare for ourselves which will wreck our lives.

When he was a lad a friend of mine was warned by his father to stay away from company that would drag him down. He told him the story of the parrot who went out flying with the crows. The poor parrot got shot by a farmer and all he could be heard saying when he hit the ground was two words; "Bad company! Bad company! Bad company!" Watch who you fly with today.

May 12th

"Do not rejoice when your enemy falls and do not let your heart be glad when he stumbles; lest the Lord see it and it displease him and he turn away his wrath from him." Proverbs 24:17-18

Now here is a difficulty. I confess that I had great difficulty in understanding this Proverb, particularly when I read in

Proverbs 25:21-22 the words "If your enemy is hungry, give him to eat and if he is thirsty, give him water to drink for so you will heap coals of fire on his head and the Lord will reward you". Is there a contradiction? Is today's Proverb suggesting that we must do nothing to arouse God's pity for our enemy?

I found the answer in what the Warden of Tyndale House, Cambridge, Derek Kidner said. He points out that if you have glee at the fall of your enemy, "Your glee may well be a more punishable sin than all the guilt of your enemy". God lifted you up when you were underserving of any lifting up so the Proverb is warning us not to gloat when our enemy falls. There, but for the grace of God, go any of us.

May 13th

"Wrath is fierce and anger is a flood, but, who can stand before jealousy?" Proverbs 27:4

You want to spoil your family life? Get jealous of someone elses. You want to wreck your business? Get jealous of anothers business success. You want to foul your work in your local church? Get jealous of some good work someone else is doing in your local church.

"Jealousy-of" will make you possessive to the point of being ridiculous. It will mean that you will not delegate and you will ruin your health by holding on too much, too long, in case someone else gets to do what you do. I've seen it and it produces some of the most pathetic people on the face of the earth.

Worse than a torrent of anger and cruelty is the sewer pipe of jealousy. It stinks and putrifies and breeds vermon in your life. If you would hold on to things then heed the words of J. G. Small's hymn which says "Nought that I have mine own to call, I hold it for the giver; my heart, my strength, my life, my all, are His, and His for ever".

If you would hold on to things hold on to them for Christ; that will make you "jealous-for" in the proper sense and get rid of your miserable "jealous-of" streak. Try it.

May 14th

"Scoffers ensnare a city but wise men turn away wrath."
Proverbs 29:8

It is very easy to knock things down. A word. A gesture. A shrug. A letter. A lifting of the finger. A joke. A sneer. A turning of the head. The world is full of scoffers.

For the last few years in my life I have visited the city of Glasgow virtually every month and I have watched the amazing progress the city has made by the efforts of an outstanding community spirit. It sprang up under the leadership of a Lord Provost who lead out under the little slogan "Glasgow smiles better".

The infectious spirit has pulled the city up by its boot straps to its position, in this year of writing, as "European City of Culture". It thoroughly deserves it.

Why not join the builders rather than the scoffers in your town or city or countryside? Extenuate the positive. Concentrate on the things that are virtuous, of good report.

I live in Belfast and I can tell you we have plenty who scoff at us. But there are things in our city which would bring admiration from any person who cares to come and see it for themselves.

Scoffers knock things down, optimists build things up. And, after all, who should be more positive than a christian?

"An angry man stirs up strife and a furious man abounds in transgression." Proverbs 29:22

It was Moffatt who paraphrased this Proverb with the memorable line "hot temper is the cause of many a sin". Are you all twisted up with bitterness and bad temper?

Let the Lord unwind those warps and think long on this little poem by Mildred M. North:

"Two cripples entered a church one day;
Crippled - but each in a different way;
One had a body strong and whole
But it sheltered a warped and twisted soul.
The other walked with a halting gait,
But his soul was 'tall and fair and straight'.
They shared a pew. They shared a book.
But on each face was a different look;
One was alight with hope and joy,
And faith that nothing could destroy.
The other joined not in prayer or hymn,
No smile relaxed his features grim.
His neighbour had wronged him; his heart was sore.
He thought of himself and nothing more.
The words that were read from the Holy Book
Struck deafened ears and a forlorn look.
To one came comfort, his soul was fed;
The other gained nothing from what was said.
Two cripples left the church that day;
Crippled - but each in a different way;
A twisted foot did one body mar,
But the twisted soul was sadder far."

"He who guards his mouth and his tongue guards his soul from troubles." Proverbs 21:23

The media love what they call a "sound bite". They wait for leaders to react hastily and then lift a single sentence and put it out across the world. They just love hasty words. They call it "good television" or whatever. It draws attention and they love to goad leaders into reacting hastily to get their "sound bites".

When we are young such things inspire us but when we are older we slowly become aware of the incredible power of words. Youth demands immediate reaction but experience teaches us caution and we begin to learn the rich rewards of self-control with our words.

I command Charles Bridges comment to you when he said: "The man who is conscious of his weakness, distrusts himself and is ready to ask and receive counsel is more likely to be led right, than he who thinks himself to be right already".

"The beginning of strife is like releasing water; therefore stop contention before a quarrel starts." Proverbs 17:14

There are few of us in the world who in childhood have not tried to build the ultimate sandcastle. There we were with our buckets and spades and as the hours passed like minutes we dug and patted those mighty bulwarks of our castle on the seashore. We had tunnels and moats and channels and great was the moment when our makeshift flag was placed on the final rampart.

We knew in our hearts, though, it wouldn't last. The tide would have us. The next day with saddened heart we went past the spot where no trace of our afternoons work could be found. So it will be if you don't abandon that contention in your life that is slowly coming to the boil. Let it go before a quarrel breaks out and all your good work be swept away. It just isn't worth it. Let the contention go. Now.

May 18th

"Whoever has no rule over his own spirit is like a city broken down, without walls." Proverbs 25:28

I had just finished preaching and sat down when a young Spaniard got into conversation with me. She was studying English in Britain and having taught the subject for some time I was interested as to which English writer impressed her most. Jane Austen? Thomas Hardy? Charles Dickens?

"Lord Byron", she said, "Because he believed in seizing the moment". He did, indeed. But to what incalculable sorrow? His pleasures led him to say that "The worm, the canker and the grief are mine alone". Seize the moment, yes, but seize it for God's glory. Let God's Holy Spirit control your impatience. Impatience thinks restraint is only a restriction and so the enemy arrives to find your walls of sure defence all down. The enemy can then take you with his bare hands. Beware of impatience.

May 19th

"Let not kindness and truth forsake you; bind them around your neck, write them on the tablet of your heart, and so find favour and high esteem in the sight of God and man." Proverbs 3:3-4

I am told that the Hebrew word "chesed" may be translated

116

into English by "kindness", "loving kindness", "mercy", "loyalty" and "righteousness". I am going to translate it uniformly as the word kindness throughout the Proverbs chosen for the next few days and pray God will use them in your life to help you overcome unrighteous anger. Let's take the first one, quoted above.

It is worth remembering that in the Old Testament the great white linen wall which surrounded the Tabernacle was held up by pillars which had a capitol on the top. In his instructions, God said that where the capitol met the pillar there was to be a fillet made of silver. It was ornamental.

The linen walls spoke of holiness and just as the pillars held up that testimony to holiness in the wilderness so must the church of Jesus Christ in our generation hold up a testimony to God's holiness. But, God was saying "Don't make what holds up that testimony look boring and unattractive. Adorn them. Make them look lovely". God likes lovely things. Don't you think kindness, adorning your every move would adorn the doctrine of God our Saviour in all things? Go on. Make the gospel on your street, at your university, on your farm, at your factory, in your office, look lovely.

May 20th

"The kind man does good for his own soul and he who is cruel troubles his own flesh." Proverbs 11:17

The deed affects the doer most. Haven't you found that? It is much more blessed to give than to receive, any day. You're doing yourself a power of good if you are kind. Deeds of kindness come back to you, in all sorts of ways. The widow of Sareptha in her kindness to Elijah, found it. Cornelius the Roman Centurion, found it, because of his alms giving. Look at the blessing Cornelius received in his life because of his alms giving! Look at the little lad who shared his lunch with Christ. He didn't know that in handing over his lunch he was going down in history!

The other side of the coin is equally as challenging. What did cruel behaviour do for Cain, for Joseph's brethren, for Achan, for Jezebel, for Judas or for Pontious Pilate?

You cannot hold a torch to light anothers path without brightening your own. Yet, remember, the kindness planned for tomorrow doesn't count for today.

May 21st

"What is desired in a man is kindness, and a poor man is better than a liar." Proverbs 19:22

Lying ranks high amongst the vices of mankind. According to one psychologist most people "tell about two lies a day, or, at least that is how many they will admit to". There is direct lying. There is professional lying. There is perjury which is lying under oath in a court. There are half truths and double meanings, flattery and exaggeration. All are associated with lying. There is even pragmatic lying which is a philosophy which says whatever works is right, that a lie isn't wrong, except when you are caught. There is, of course, lying even in the advertising you see around you. Worst of all there is lying to God (See Acts 5:23).

Lying is wrong. Always wrong. It affects us, it affects others and it affects our relationship with God. Satan is the father of lying and kindness is not his desire. It is what God desires in us, though. If your tongue is ruled by the law of kindness you will not lie to God nor man. Like perfume to flower so is kindness to speech. May your speech be saturated with kindness, today.

May 22nd

"Open your mouth for the speechless ... plead the cause of the poor and needy." Proverbs 31:8

Now there is kindness. All over your community are those who are speechless. They haven't got the courage nor are they articulate enough to speak up for themselves. Their circumstances have bowed them down and they are unable to do anything about it.

Do you speak for them? Do you plead their cause? They are all around you. Above all what greater area of concern could we have in the nation than for those little speechless ones whose parents are incredibly selfish? I had to plead for one with its mother who rang me on the phone the other day wanting to abort it for no other reason than that she didn't want it. She said she was a christian, too. May God give us the opportunity to speak up for the speechless ones in this frighteningly selfish age. Be kind to dumb people.

May 23rd

"On her tongue is the law of kindness." Proverbs 31:26

Today I want to share some words from Florence Littauer with you. Florence is one of my favourite writers on the subject of marriage and she has this message; "Men ... when you criticise us, we get worse. When you compliment us, we get better. When you try to change us, we won't budge. When you accept us as we are, we try to improve. When you don't help us, we are mad because you're sitting. When you will insist, we insist that you sit down. When you pick on the children, we think you hate us. When you are positive and encouraging, we know you love us. When you are too busy to listen, we nag and ramble. When you set aside time to converse, we condense our comments. We really are so easy to please when you love us. You can turn our whole lives around when you let us know we come first".

May 24th

"Will they not go astray who devise evil? But kindness and truth belong to those who devise good." Proverbs 14:22

An amazing number of people in this world set out to do evil to others. They think evil. There are others who, by God's grace, know Christ as Saviour and set out to devise good. Which are you?

I love the story of Charlie Steinmetz who, though small in stature, was a genius when it came to things electrical. No one knew it better than Henry Ford.

One day Henry's automobile assemble plant at Dearborn, Michigan went dead. One mechanic after another found it impossible to locate the source of the problem. Eventually Charlie was contacted and after he had pressed a few buttons here and messed about with a few wires here and there and tinkered with this and that, he threw the main switch and the lights came back on.

A few days later he sent Henry Ford a bill for $10,000. Henry sent the bill back saying "Doesn't it seem a little steep to charge me $10,000 for tinkering around with a few wires and switches?" Charlie re-wrote the bill and sent it back. It read: For tinkering around on the motors $10; for knowing where to tinker $9,990.

Christian, you know where it's at. It's no $10,000 question is it? Read today's Proverb and go and put it into action.

"Whoever digs a pit will fall into it and he who rolls a stone will have it rolled back on him." Proverbs 26:27

This is a warning. Are you tempted to be unkind? Are you tempted to give way to unrighteous anger and to set a trap for the one who has hurt you? Watch it. You will fall into the hole you have dug.

Think of the hole Joseph's brothers dug for him and the stone they set rolling against him. The day came when they fell far deeper than any desert hole and that deed they did came crashing back on them with incredible voracity. Only Joseph's kindness saved them from extinction. Life is strewn with examples of people whose lives have been wrecked in the pits they dug for others and fell into themselves. Watch how you use that spade.

"If your enemy is hungry, give him bread to eat; and if he is thirsty, give him water to drink; for so you will heap coals of fire on his head, and the Lord will reward you.".Proverbs 25:21-22

In the first years of the 4th century there lived a christian called Phocas who lived in a cottage outside the city gate. He made no secret of his faith and hundreds have tasted the simple hospitality of his cottage home. When the Diocletian persecution broke out the Lictoras were dispatched in haste to Sinope to identify and execute him on the spot. So it happened that, tired with their journey, the executioners were nearing the gate of Sinope one hot afternoon when they were hailed from a cottage garden by an old man who begged them to pause a while and refresh themselves. They did so. "What is your business?", said their host. They told him they were seeking a certain Phocas. Did their host know him? He was a dangerous christian and had to be executed immediately. "I know him well", said Phocas. "He is quite near", they said, "Let us attend to it in the morning".

When his guests retired Phocas sat thinking. To escape would be easy. He had only to go to his fellow christians and they would hide him. When the persecution was over he could emerge again. If he ran, would it be cowardly? But what of the executioners? Decent fellows as they seemed; just doing their duty? Their own lives might be forfeit for his.

When his guests rose the next morning he told them who he was and history tells us that they stood "motionless" in astonishment. They shrank from a deed so foul upon a man so kind. He overcame their reluctance. Death, he said, had no terrors for him. They had their duty to do and he had nothing but love in his heart for them. A sword swept, and all that was mortal of Phocas mingled with the garden he had loved so well.

May 27th

"A friend loves at all times." Proverbs 17:17

Dr. W. E. Sangster tells that as a small boy he was very fearful of his stern father. "I sometimes hesitated to ask him things I dearly wished and would confide my hopes to my mother instead. Always - or nearly always - she said, 'Ask him'. She knew the character of his heart better than I did and she believed also in the direct approach.

I have remembered the advice through the years, both in my dealings with God and man. When foolish hesitations have hampered my converse with heaven and with my fellows, I have remembered the loving admonition 'Ask Him'. So I have asked God for men and men for God. It has usually been easier than I feared. Times without number tremulous souls have as much as admitted that they were waiting to be asked. I dread to think how many I have failed in that way".

Let us heed Dr. Sangster's warning and if we would truly love folk at all times let us ask the Lord for guidance as to how we might show his love toward them. He will not fail to guide us.

May 28th

"He who follows righteousness and kindness finds life, righteousness and honour."Proverbs 21:21

In a certain German town a lady found a basket on her doorstep and in the basket was a pigeon. On a note inside a message was written that if the lady did not fasten a certain sum of money to the clip on the pigeon's leg and release the bird immediately her home would be burned down that night.

The lady informed the police and they chartered two aeroplanes, tied a streaming ribbon to the bird's neck and released it instructing the pilots to pursue it. It flew on a direct course to another town and down to a loft by one of its houses.

The police dashed to the house and apprehended the two men who were feverishly untying the telltale ribbon. They protested saying that the bird was not theirs. "It just flew into our loft", they said; "It's not our bird". "Very well", said the police, "we will test that". They ordered the pigeon to be taken away and released from a distant spot, and it came home. A second time it was taken away and a second time it came home. It even came home a third time and every time it deepened the certainty of their guilt. Finally they broke down and confessed.

Sin is like that, it always finds you out. On the other hand if you follow today's Proverb life, righteousness and honour will find you. Wouldn't you rather have those two lovely qualities pursuing you than sin?

May 29th

"Like a flitting sparrow." Proverbs 26:2

I took her funeral service one day and only one mourner turned up. The lady had died two years before and had bequeathed her body for the purposes of scientific research. I wondered what I would say to that one lonely mourner and then I thought of the sparrow. I spoke to him of how sparrows fall and no one notices. That is no one, except God. God's eye was with us in that service. God knew. God understood. Millions may one day thank God for that lady because of some medical discovery through her selfless act. Meantime we honoured her together that lonely mourner and me, and God. Be kind to sparrows.

May 30th

"Through wisdom a house is built, and by understanding it is established." Proverbs 24:3

Yesterday we thought of sparrows, today I want to think of rooks. I have always thought unkindly of rooks. They always appear to me to be useless creatures. I have recently been made to change my unkind mind. There is no better natural barometer than a rook. They make excellent forecasters for all weathers. When rooks fly from their nests and fly straight, umbrellas and raincoats can be left at home all day. Should the rooks twist and turn on leaving their nests, rough weather is approaching. However, if gales are on the way rooks stay by their nests, screaming raucously.

When those rooks are leaving the rookery in the morning and then hang about, feeding on the roadside and on village streets, it will rain. The twig nests are also very important, as it is said that high nests mean a good summer. Low nests suggest the destruction of the old nest sites during winter gales and so building lower, on more secure branches, can indicate a particular weather pattern. So, don't think unkindly of the old rook, even he builds even his house with wisdom given to him by God. Let us do the same.

May 31st

"A man's gift makes room for him, and brings him before great men". Proverbs 18:16

We live in an age of manipulators. All around us people are shoving and pushing for all kinds of things. They think if they shout loud enough and pull enough strings it will get them to where they want to go. They would be better heeding today's Proverb. It is a much kinder and better way.

There lives a christian man in Edinburgh whom I had the privilege of staying with recently. He told me that he had made it a rule in his work life never to manipulate his way. He and his wife decided that they would follow whatever the boss told him to do. He was in telecommunications and one day the boss asked him to move to Glasgow. Now Hedley and his wife did not want to move to Glasgow but following their rule they obeyed. A short time later Dr. Billy Graham arrived in Glasgow at the Kelvin Hall and brought forward the idea of relaying his evangelistic meetings all over the country by landline relays. It had never been done before but the new Deputy Manager of Telecommunications in the city of Glasgow was my friend Hedley. I shall never forget the glow upon his face as he told me how he set to work for Billy and his friends and an incalculable host of people were reached with the Gospel as a result. He was very glad he had not manipulated his way.

Did he stand before great men? Well,my friend eventually rose to become the chief in telecommunications in Scotland and was put in charge of all the telecommunications at Balmoral Castle whenever the King held his court there. I must say I spent a delightful time in Edinburgh with Mr. Revell as I sought to communicate the King of Kings messages from the word of God. My friend was in fact a living example of what I was trying to preach. Selah.

JUNE

June brides. They are beautiful and numerous. Here is some advice for them from the Book of Proverbs. It will help older brides too, and, if followed, will result in fewer marriages breaking down. We shall seek to balance this advice with proverbs on the qualities a husband should have. Here is a chance for monogomous relationships to shine in a new way. We don't want the jeweller's shop in your town to hang up a sign like the one I heard of which read, "We rent wedding rings". Let's put that kind of renting business out of business.

June 1st

'A man who isolates himself seeks his own desire." Proverbs 18:1

The story is told of a man who was constantly going out to church services. One evening his wife stopped him and asked him where he was going. He replied that he was going down to the local church where a missionary was showing a set of slides entitled "Going through Africa with a camel". "You are not going", she said. "Why not?", he asked. "Because you are going into the kitchen to go through China with a dishcloth!"

June 2nd

"A continual dripping on a very rainy day and a contentious woman are alike whoever restrains her restrains the wind and grasps oil with his right hand." Proverbs 27:15-16

The epitaph read "Beneath this sod a lump of clay lies Arabella Young who on the 31st May began to hold her tongue". If Arabella was contentious then somebody must have felt the effect of her tongue. Is there anything that changes quicker than a woman who stops scolding to answer the phone? As sure as the constant dripping of water would wear even a rock away so a woman's tongue, if she is contentious, will wear her husband away too. Beware, fellows, of "the drip" and marry her not.

June 3rd

"As a ring of gold in a swine's snout, so is a lovely woman who lacks discretion." Proverbs 11:22

Here is beauty and the beast. This Proverb certainly does not mince matters. Discretion means right judgement, cautious and wise behaviour. Good looks are enhanced by it and are positively a disadvantage without it. How well I remember an older lady who was parking her car one day. Another very attractive lady driver behaved very badly towards her. The older lady let her park and then as she walked past she said to her quietly "I thought you were a lady when I first saw you, now, I know you're not". Drive carefully, good lookin'.

June 4th

"He who finds a wife finds a good thing, and obtains favour from the Lord." Proverbs 18:22

Next to wisdom, the best of God's blessings any man can have is a good wife. Do you appreciate her, sir? Who says the honeymoon must end? The very God of heaven has given her to you. Remember, then, the down to earth advice of one Ogden Nash. Ogden knew a thing or two and was a wordsmith who seldom missed his target. He advised that if you would keep love in the loving cup, "When you're wrong admit it and when you are right, shut up".

June 5th

"Can one walk on hot coals and his feet not be seared? So is he who goes into his neighbour's wife; whoever touches her shall not be innocent ... he who does so destroys his own soul."
Proverbs 6:27-32

Affairs. They abound in our nation and are categorically condemned by God. H. N. Wright has 8 questions to ask those who are wanting to know the answer to the question "Am I leaning towards an affair?" I leave them with you. Let us make sure that we are not helping to create the conditions for an affair in our own life or in that of our partners.

1. Do you have the feeling you are simply going through the motions of a marriage?

2. Are you creating excuses to continually visit with someone in your work or social environment?

3. How do you handle repetitive contact with a particular person in a working, social or sporting situation?

4. Do you find yourself pre-occupied with your thoughts about another person?

5. Why are you exchanging a gift with a person of the opposite sex?

6. How important has the telephone become in your relationship with a friend outside your marriage?

7. Are you consciously putting yourself into situations where you can increase your chances of meeting someone who might become more than a friend?

8. If the eyes are the window to the brain, what message does the look in our eye give to another person? What do our non-verbals say to others? Our body language makes up 50%

of our communication and can transmit messages which are quite obvious.

By Way of Explanation

I once received a letter from a single girl a few days before I was to speak at a public meeting on the subject of "singleness". "Please Derick", she wrote, "Don't just get up and tell us we have the Lord and can be as happy single as married because for most of us it's not true. After a while you begin to feel there is something wrong with you. And you get called 'old maid', 'on the shelf', 'hard to please', 'bad tempered', 'odd'. For some people it's a source of wonderment. Others try to tell you how better off you are. There is nothing so annoying as married people telling single people how awful it is to be married, tied down, committed. Most of us would love some of those problems. Most people make light of it all and are ignorant of the problems single people face."

Well, I hope I'm not ignorant of the problems of single people. I am certainly sure that God can give them a rich, full life without marriage if that is His will for them.

For the next few days we are going to study the qualities of the ideal woman of Proverbs 31. Out of the list of 24 qualities only 4 or 5 have to do specifically with her married state. So we are going to skip the references to her husband and children and concentrate on what made her so valuable. Whether you are married or single may these Proverbs be a blessing to you.

June 6th

"She ... willingly works with her hands." Proverbs 31:13

Have you ever noticed how people enjoy being around someone who works cheerfully and willingly? What about

132

Mrs. Matilda Rogers of Waynesville, North Carolina? When she reached her 111th birthday she said her recipe for longevity was "plenty of hard work and no worry". Mrs. Rogers, the matriarch of a clan of 284 living descendants had 5 sons, 4 daughters, 65 grandchildren, 79 great-grandchildren, 125 great-great-grandchildren and to top it all 6 new great-great-great-grandchildren born since she turned 110 years. Her oldest child is a son of 92!

Proverbs 10:4 tells us that the person who "deals with a slack hand becomes poor but the hand of the diligent makes one rich. He who gathers in summer is a wise son, but he who sleeps in harvest is a son who causes shame".

A willing, cheerful hard working person is worth knowing. If you and I are lazy and miserable is it any wonder people don't want to know us? This lady willingly works with her hands.

The number of people who are unemployed, you know, isn't as great as the number who aren't working. Think about it.

June 7th

"She brings her food from afar." Proverbs 31:14

This lady is a good shopper. It was not easy for her. In our day it is no easier to balance a family budget when supermarket trolleys often travel at £100 an hour! Yet, poor management displeases the Lord. Nowhere in Scripture do we ever read that financial success is suspect. Management and discipline planning go hand-in-hand. Unwise overspending breaks relationships and lives and we must never become a slave of the lender. "The borrower is servant to the lender", says the Proverb.

Is it wrong to borrow? It has been pointed out that when the Scripture says "Owe no man anything" the imperative is in the present tense. The thought is "don't keep on owing". It means that we must pay our debts and not pile up back-to-back loans so that we are never free of them.

Keep short accounts, and you'll be able to bring plenty of food from afar.

June 8th

"She rises while it is yet night and provides food for her household." Proverbs 21:15

The feminists would get pretty wild if this Proverb only applied to women; it doesn't. Other Scriptures show very clearly that men are also called to go beyond mere duty. "Provides food for her household" carries the idea of providing "what is appointed". In sickness, trauma and tragedy, immediate calls upon our help can often come in the night. God's grace is available to help us meet them.

It was the British Prime Minister, Pitt, who said about another M.P.; "Dundas is no orator but he would go out with you in any kind of weather". Let's have more folk like Dundas.

June 9th

"She considers a field and buys it." Proverbs 31:16

Notice this lady does not fritter away her hard earned cash on non-essentials. She shrewdly makes a good investment. Was it not the Saviour who asked the man who had hidden his talent as to why he didn't put his money on deposit so that when his master returned he could have collected it with interest? Initiative in investment is God honouring.

How we budget, save, spend and invest is just as important to God as how we worship. This lady's wise investment brought God as much pleasure as her attendance at her place of worship. Investing money is just as important in the christian life as our evangelism. There is no secular - sacred distinction in the matter. Let's not make any.

June 10th

"She perceives that her merchandise is good." Proverbs 31:18

This lady took pride in her work. Why shouldn't you and I do the same? Here in Northern Ireland there lived a very gracious lady who was much loved and respected. Unfortunately she was killed recently in a car accident and this province is a lot poorer without her. Her name was the Duchess of Westminster.

She had arranged once to put a stain glass window in a certain building and, one day, out walking in casual clothes she went to see how the workmen were getting on. Chatting with one of them she was told that the work was for "an old doll with a lot of money to spend"! Can you imagine the consternation of the workman when he found out who he had been talking to? The Duchess didn't let him put her off her good work, though. She perceived that her merchandise was good. Let them talk. She went on her way with a smile.

June 11th

"She stretches out her hand to the distaff and her hand holds the spindle ... she makes tapestry for herself; her clothing is fine linen and purple.". Proverbs 31:19-22

Translators are unsure of the meaning of the word "distaff" in this Proverb but it has been given as "she stretches out her hand to the mending". Some say that the point of the Proverb is that this lady can afford the very best but surely the point of the Proverb is that beautiful things need not necessarily be expensive.

I went to a beautiful exhibition of flowers recently but one exhibit disappointed me greatly; they had sprayed the flowers with paint! Why, an old bit of driftwood picked up from the shore and some tastefully arranged flowers can make a display fit for a king. You don't need to paint it!

I know some women who make the most beautiful clothes which would rival any designer label. Creativity has been ruined by television. Let's live life instead of just watching it. This lady makes tapestry "for herself". There is a personal pleasure in creativity that there is in nothing else. We were created in God's image and creativity is part of our nature; don't ignore it.

June 12th

"She extends her hand to the poor, yes, she reaches out her hands to the needy." Proverbs 31:20

There are always people who are poor around us and not just financially. There are people who are poor in friendship. Extend your hand to them. Yours may be the first hand they have shaken in a week, or a year. There are people who are poor in their quality of life; a big percentage of our children, for example, live in broken homes before they reach the age of 18. "Latch key" children are everywhere. The family needs help.

I find as I travel that there are people all over the world who are very poor regarding the lovely treasures of Scripture. They are near to a spiritual goldmine but no one has bothered to point it out to them. If you have Bible knowledge; share it, don't hoard it. I find that young christians have a lot of zeal but can't possibly have a lot of knowledge at their age and at the same time I find older christians who have plenty of knowledge gathered through the years but unfortunately they no longer have the zeal. True? If you find poverty or need on your path today, reach out and help.

June 13th

"Strength and honour are her clothing." Proverbs 31:25

Have you seen any leading articles recently in "Vogue" or "McCalls" on the importance of wearing strength and honour? You couldn't wear anything more becoming. This lady did not just wear fine linen and purple; did she?

This generation of ours is over stimulated. They are bombarded by noise and raucous advertising compelling them to wear this, try that, go here, stay there. Calmness, serenity and inner strength are not for sale. They come, ultimately from a quiet trust in God that, no matter what, He is working out a great purpose in our lives. Always.

June 14th

"She will rejoice in time to come." Proverbs 31:25

I like the translation of this Proverb which says, "She can afford to laugh, looking ahead". Are you deeply depressed? Are you thinking it's not worth it and are you ready to quit? Are you feeling that things will never pick up and the future is bleak? Christian, you must never be afraid to trust an unknown future to a known God.

Look at the God you know. Has He ever failed you? Does He keep His promises? Has He ever made you ashamed of Him? If His promises for your future were to disappoint you He says He would be ashamed to be called your God (see Hebrews 11:13-16). Abraham left his country behind to go

137

to a city God had prepared for him. He had opportunity to go back but he didn't. He was not disappointed and neither will you be.

June 15th

"She ... does not eat the bread of idleness." Proverbs 31:27

Have you ever known any man or woman to succeed in any business or in any profession who was jealous of the hours they gave to their job? It's a bit like the sign found on an office bulletin board which read "Would you like to find out what it's like to be a member of a minority group? Try putting in an honest days work occasionally". You wouldn't want to be like the bees who went on strike would you? Heard about them? They went on strike for shorter flowers and more honey!

Idleness is a curse. It will lead you to boredom and mischief. "Far and away the best prize that life offers", said Theodore Roosevelt, "is the chance to work hard at work worth doing". The lady in our Proverb would agree.

June 16th

"For the commandment is a lamp and the law is light ... to keep you from the evil woman, from the flattering tongue of a seductress. Do not lust after her beauty in your heart nor let her alure you with her eyelids." Proverbs 6:23-25

Not all women are like the lady we have thought about over the last few days. The evil woman described here is full of flattery. Her words are smooth and slippery and she is out to wreck lives. Inhale the perfume of her flattery and she will have you at her mercy. Flattery is her weapon. What is flattery? It is often the art of telling a person exactly what he thinks of himself. Even a phrase like "Oh! I know you are the kind of man who can't be flattered", is flattery.

If you come across flattery today, ignore it and remember, christian, God's estimate of us. "Christ died for the ungodly" the Scriptures tell us. Our sin would have dammed us in Hell. Make no mistake about it. Apart from what we have and are in Christ we would have perished.

Let Calvary temper all the praise you get and teach you to ignore flattery.

June 17th

"Treasure my commands within you, keep my commands and live, and my law as the apple of your eye ... say to wisdom 'You are my sister' and call understanding your nearest kin that they may keep you from the immoral woman." Proverbs 7:1-5

This is a very vivid description of the protection the word of God gives us in our lives if we heed it. It will protect us just like eyelids protect "the apple" of our eye. The apple of the eye refers to the pupil of the eye.

The pupil is the black dot in the centre of the eye and its job is to let light in. The iris, or circle of colour in the eye controls the amount of light let in by controlling the pupil.

The iris controls tiny muscles which close the pupil in bright light when less is needed and open it in dull light when more is needed. The eye is a very delicate instrument and needs the greatest possible protection. Eyelids automatically close when anything approaches too near.

Let God's word protect you today when temptation approaches and whatever you do don't despise it.

June 18th

"For at the window of my house I look through my lattice, and saw among the simple, I perceived among the youths, a young man devoid of understanding. Passing along the street near her corner; and he took the path to her house in the twilight, in the evening, in the black and dark night and there a woman met him with the attire of a prostitute and a crafty heart." Proverbs 7:6-10

The next few days Proverbs may seem irrelevant to you. They are not irrelevant to God. This part of His word is as inspired as any other part and we must not ignore it because it deals with a highly obnoxious subject of prostitution.

Proverbs show us how this young man got into the trap of this evil woman. He wandered into temptation. Notice that, place (he was in a dangerous place) and, time (it was as dark as night) combined forces to bring him down.

Just because he was in the wrong place at the wrong time, though, doesn't mean he should have necessarily fallen. His problem was that he was aimless and the woman about to tempt him, wasn't. Aimlessness brings more trouble on our heads than we could ever imagine. Wherever you go today, even in broad daylight, don't go there aimlessly. There are people around who are not aimless.

June 19th

"And there a woman met him, with the attire of a prostitute, and a crafty heart. She was loud and rebellious, her feet would not stay at home. At times she was outside, at times in the open square, lurking at every corner. So she caught him and kissed him; with an impudent face she said to him ... I have found you." Proverbs 7:10-15

How free and easy this woman looks! Not for her the attire

of a mother, weary at the end of the day after caring for her children and her husband.

Here is no reality, here is falsity. Why? She might be dressed, sure, but notice our English expression, she is "dressed to kill". Kill she will; hearts, homes and lives.

The free easy and carefree outward look guards a hard, un-yielding, close, secretive, crafty heart.

As Kidner puts it, "Outwardly she keeps nothing back, inwardly she gives nothing away. It will be an unequal contest".

Her kiss is the kiss of death. Her proffered love is a lie. Don't believe her. Ever.

June 20th

"Let us delight ourselves with love. For my husband is not at home; he has gone on a long journey." Proverbs 7:19

The adultress lady of today's text says that adultery is love. Is not this still the modern cry?

A wife runs off with someone and says "But I love him". What kind of love is it that would divide children, alienate a husband and wreck a home? That kind of "love" is a fiend, is it not? It is not love at all; it is downright selfishness.

I have counselled in this area and heard a christian who had broken the marriage bond to get involved with someone else say how he wanted to win his new partner for Christ.

What kind of Christ did he want to win her for? It was certainly not the Christ of the New Testament.

The commandment "Thou shalt not commit adultery" still stands.

"With her enticing speech she caused him to yield, with her flattering lips she seduced him. Immediately he went after her as an ox goes to the slaughter, or as a fool to the correction of the stocks, till an arrow struck his liver. As a bird hastens to the snare, he did not know it would take his life." Proverbs 7:21-23

"Amazingly", says the straight talking Mrs. Littauer, "most men choose women who are just like we used to be before they wore us down trying to re-make us". She points out that it is hard for a mother surrounded by screaming children to look as glamorous as the secretary who spent a quiet hour on her make-up. "It's wrong for a man", she says, "to reject a wife who has struggled through poor times and put up with the quirks of his mother just as he makes it to the top and can travel to Tahiti".

I agree. And when he does fall for the seductress he thinks it is falling for something as soft as down, not realising that before it is finished the thing will be a flaming vulture. As our Proverb teaches, like an unwitting beast going to the slaughter or a bird lighting in a snare so the foolish man will be caught by the seductress. She will destroy his life. Repeat. His life. Fancy an arrow in your liver, sir? No? Then do not go down her path.

"Do not let your heart turn aside to her ways, do not stray into her paths; for she has cast down many wounded, and all who were slain by her were strong men. Her house is the way to hell, descending to the chambers of death." Proverbs 7:25-27

In all of the 365 Proverbs I will deal with in this book this little passage is the most frightening. I wish I could write these words across every pornagraphic magazine that winks at the millions who pass through our airports or local newspaper shops. I wish I could put it in an neon sign across every red-light district in the great cities of the world. I wish I could put it across every dirty film beamed across the nation and print it in every filthy novel published. Sad to say with the incredible scenes of freedom in Eastern Europe that we have witnessed recently the new influx of all the materials just mentioned that is pouring into the newly untangled nations is beyond comprehension.

How do we guard against it? First by guarding our minds; "do not let your heart (i.e. your mind) turn aside to her". Second, keep away; "do not stray into her path". Third, keep your eye, not on her but on the fearful causalties whose lives she has blasted. They live in the "chambers of death". Follow these three guidelines and you will never stray.

June 23rd

"Her husband also, he praises her." Proverbs 31:28

O.K. So we have looked at the Proverbs dealing with the ideal woman and her exact counterpoint. Now, let's look at husbands as June days slip into summer. Let's balance the teaching by putting a few mottos on the desks of busy husbands. Just because you sit in a board room all day, sir, doesn't mean you have to sit in a bored room all night.

Often as I travel I hear men criticise their wives. How boring it is! They criticise the food she cooks, they nag at her for this and that. What they are doing is actually trying to convince others of their competence by cutting down their wives. Such a man is a bore to be with because he is only building up his own ego at the expense of browbeating his poor wife. He thinks he is impressing others with how tolerant and competent he is in comparison with the poor wife he has had to live with all of these years. None of us are impressed. Give honour to your wife. Praise her.

June 24th

"A slothful man buries his hand in the bowl and will not so much as bring it to his mouth again." Proverbs 19:24

Don't you think some husbands are like the comically extreme character in our Proverb? They will not follow through nor initiate. Here is a husband who leaves child raising to his wife and then complains that she dominates! If you don't bother to lead your family to church attendance is it any wonder your wife becomes the spiritual leader in your house? If your wife reads God's Word and prays with them and you don't bother, is it any wonder they look to her for spiritual guidance. Who initiates family holidays or outings in your house? Who makes the major decisions, after consultation in your family circle? Husband, stand up and be a man. That is what you were called to be. Not a chauvinist but a leader, an initiator, a decision maker. This is time for action.

June 25th

"Drink water from your own cistern and running water from your own well." Proverbs 5:15

It is amazing how many men are still emotionally tied to their mothers or fathers. They can hardly make a single move as adults without consulting their parents. Years into their married life some men wouldn't take time off to go to their children's school prize day or whatever but immediately their mother rings they are round to her like a shot. They are still emotionally, physically and financially tied to their parents.

We are not talking about miserable isolationism but we are saying that it is up to a husband to "leave" his parents and "cleave" to his wife. In any disputes allegiance must be to our partner. The Bible teaches that we must honour our mother and father but when we marry their authority must not establish our new home or the decisions made in it. I have literally seen people prematurely old because they did not get the balance right. Don't be one of them.

June 26th

"Rejoice with the wife of your youth ... always be enraptured with her love." Proverbs 5:18-19

Did you notice that little word "rejoice", men, in today's Proverb? Not "quarrel" with your wife, not "endure life" with your wife, not "neglect" your wife, not "be bored" with your wife but "rejoice" with her. You ardently chose her in your youth, now as the years pass "rejoice" with her.

Don't you think your wife will respond to being loved? If she knows that you love her she can put up with much around her that is overwhelming and frightening. If you speak kindly to her and care for her it will make an enormous difference in your relationship.

Is your wife really in love with you? Next time you are out with a married couple count how many times they have direct eye contact. You'd be amazed how many wives divert their eyes away from their husbands. It has to do with lack of respect and years of neglect.

"For the ways of man are before the eyes of the Lord and he ponders all his paths." Proverbs 5:21

The Lord's eyes are not diverted from a husband's behaviour. How do you think the Lord feels if a husband is always admiring what other women wear, what other women say, what other women do and never admires what his wife wears, what his wife says or, what his wife does? The thing must displease him just as much as it displeases the unnoticed wife. The Bible commands husbands to give honour to their wives. That means they are not to spend their time always giving honour to other people's wives.

Mind you, it works the other way too, doesn't it? I heard of a speaker who received a compliment from someone who heard him speak at a public meeting. His wife had not complimented him for anything in years so he thought he would reveal to her what his listener had said. He pointed out that the lady had complimented him for being a very "warm" speaker. "That means", said his wife, "you are not so hot". On such rocks do marriages perish.

June 28th

"... put your hand on your mouth." Proverbs 30:32

In the city where I live a wall was recently built to divide two communities, one supposedly economically poorer than the other. It had nothing to do with politics, that wall, it had to do with snobbery. The residents of the economically poorer area went wild, and, no wonder. "Something there is that does not love a wall", said Robert Frost. Some husbands build a wall when communicating with their wives by con-

146

stantly interrupting them. It gets so bad at times that the interrupted wife is so afraid to open her mouth she holds back and builds a wall of silence.

"Last Wednesday we went out in the late morning"; "Early afternoon", he interrupts. "We had coffee"; "I had tea", he adds. "An hour later"; "It was actually 40 minutes", "Tell it yourself", she bursts out! Could you blame her?

So, for once, husband, if you are guilty of constantly interrupting your wife, put your hand on your mouth, for once.

June 29th

"They love him who speaks right." Proverbs 16:13

Do you ever think that you said one thing, husband, and it came across as another?

I mean to ask this question, positively. When you said "I'm sorry", to your wife that was what you said but your wife heard the words "I love you". When you said "I'll run you to the bus" to your teenage daughter, father, she actually heard you saying "I care". When you said "I'll go fishing with you, son", your son heard you say "I really want to be with you for an afternoon, son". Got it?

Words of love and kindness are not always said directly but they are heard. Loud and clear.

June 30th

"The leech has two daughters, crying, 'Give! Give!'"
Proverbs 30:15

The leech lives of other people's blood; its identical twins are no different. The context of this Proverb is the person of

147

unending ambition. What is the answer to such a miserable motivation?

When the fomerly blind Bartimaeus opened his eyes to see the Lord Jesus standing before him, I wonder did he get a shock? Did he expect to see God in Christ stained with dust on his way to Calvary, the servant king? One thing about Bartimaeus is absolutely certain; he never begged again. He never said, leech-like, "Give me! Give me! Give me!" any more. Why? The Scriptures say that "He followed Jesus in the way". What way? Christ's way: the way of service. Selah, men and women selah. Let your marriage be filled with such service and it will never founder.

July

The lazy, hazy, days of summer are upon us. This year, though, as I have been writing this book, I have had the interesting experience of having had to go through two winters. Just as we are coming into summer in the United Kingdom I have had to leave it and go into two months of a New Zealand winter! So, for me, it's back to warmer clothes and ice and snow.

Still, there are the compensations of those wonderful natural thermal pools in New Zealand to look forward to. At night we luxuriate in them under the Southern Star with frost on the ground all around us. Winter or summer, though, we must be careful not to let laziness swamp us. Nothing can be more dangerous. Laziness can undermine the whole quality of life. Let's see what the Proverbs have to say on the subject; they will keep us on the right track through July days.

July 1st

"Go to the ant, you sluggard, consider her ways and be wise, which having no captain, overseer or ruler, provides her supplies in the summer and gathers her food in the harvest." Proverbs 6:6-8

Is your work lonely? Do you serve the Lord Jesus in an obscure place? Is there no one to report to, oversee, or guide your work? Do you sometimes feel like saying "Who cares whether I witness or not? Who cares whether I read my Bible or pray or work for the Lord? Bother, I'll pull back!"

Be careful. Laziness can make you live for the present and not care for the souls of people around you. Let us never forget that life is very short and eternity is very long. The person who seeks to win souls for the Lord is wise. By evangelism and christian work you are laying up great treasure for the future. No earthly eye may care much about your work but the heart of your Lord does. Don't pull back. The ant doesn't need an overseer, a captain or a ruler to tell it that the future counts. It beavers away in summer preparing for future days.

Learn from the little creature.

July 2nd

"How long will you slumber, O sluggard? When will you rise from your sleep?" Proverbs 6:9-10

It is worth remembering that even if you lie in your bed all day, the world will still continue to corkscrew through space. Time will move on whatever you do or don't do. I know that you may not want to face another day. I know that you may have been hurt or criticised or bludgeoned by people out there but a lazy "see if I care" attitude won't solve things.

There is no question that millions of people could see incredible things happen in their lives if only they would make the most of the opportunities God puts in their way. Sleeping all the time won't help. Nor will a tranquillizer. Stir up the gift of God that is within you. Let them talk and say whatever they want. When the lemonade is still sour it is because the sugar is at the bottom and needs to be stirred. "Some day" and "one of these days" are the sluggards favourite words. If it is worth seeing or hearing or doing, get out there and see and hear and do it.

Every day holds immense opportunities for great and true fortune. Don't sleep those opportunities away. Wake up! Today is the day.

July 3rd

"A little sleep, a little slumber, a little folding of the hands to sleep, so shall your poverty come on you like a robber and your need like an armed man." Proverbs 6:10-11

The parish minister showed me around the parish church building at Crimmond, Aberdeenshire. He had been having a busy day and I deeply appreciated the fact that he took time off for a few moments to show me around. The clock on the tower caught my attention. It is famous for having, as a result of an error, 61 minutes to the hour. In 1949 when the clock was being repainted, the extra minute was removed, but this caused such a furore that the extra minute was restored. The text on the clock reads "The hour cometh". The hour might be a minute later at Crimmond but it comes all the same!

The hour of poverty can come, too. If we let our time drift, if we do not have our time strictly arranged, laziness will take root and sooner or later poverty will have us and strip us of everything. "Rest and play", said Harold Mayfield, "are the desserts of life. Work is the meal. It is only a child who dreams of a diet of dessert alone".

July 4th

"He who heeds the word wisely will find good, and whoever trusts in the Lord, happy is he." Proverbs 16:20

On American Independence Day I think it would be good to quote a very famous American christian who went to be with Christ, recently. His name was Vance Havner and he was a great christian communicator right into a very ripe old age.

People kept asking him if he would like to live his life over again. "Live my life over when I am this near home?", he said, "I'm not interested. Who wants to go back? Some of us may leave this life under difficult circumstances, but one thing is certain: God may put some of us to bed in the dark, but He will get us all up in the morning. And that is what I'm looking for. God is up all night. He's always available. I think of the old bishop who could not sleep, so at two in the morning he got up and started reading his Bible. He came to where it says, 'He that keepeth Israel neither slumbers nor sleeps'.

He said, 'Well, Lord, if you're sitting up, I'm going to bed. Goodnight.'"

July 5th

"The slothful man says 'There is a lion outside! I shall be slain in the streets." Proverbs 22:13

I have seen it, even in spiritual things. Churches, and individuals in them, "hug the coastline" using the excuse that they fear all sorts of things and as a result they never experience the blessing that would have been theirs if only they had ventured farther out for God.

What if Moses had slothfully lazed about in his privileged position in the Easy Street or Egypt? He could have continued using all sorts of excuses for not getting involved in God's plan for his life. If he had continued to say "Lord, here am I send Aaron", he would never have seen the Red Sea open or manna fall from Heaven or have had those wonderful talks with God on Sinai. Are you spiritually slothful? God alone knows what you are missing.

Waken up and get going!

"The sluggard is wiser in his own eyes than seven men who can answer sensibly." Proverbs 26:16

Sluggardsville has all the answers. In that town they know how to dodge every suggestion of hard work and commitment to excellence. I didn't visit the place, today. In fact this morning I visited a lady who is so paralysed she can't even wipe away tears from her own eyes. There were some in mine as I lunched with her at the headquarters of her organization.

On the walls were the beautiful paintings she had painted with a paint brush in her mouth. Around her were a dedicated staff answering hundreds of thousands of letters from people who write to her from all over the world about their troubles. On the wall was a citation mentioning that Christmas cards carrying her paintings had sold over 15 million copies. On the shelves around her were copies of the books she had written. As we spoke together of the Lord Jesus her face lit up with joy. I have seldom spent a more inspiring hour in my life than I did with that lady. Smart talkin' sluggards abound but Joni Eareckson Tada isn't one of them. Whose faith follow.

"The soul of a sluggard desires and has nothing; but the soul of the dilligent shall be made rich." Proverbs 13:4

A great principle for all family and public life is that present conduct determines future conditions. In life we blindly call certain moments great and feel they have influenced our whole lives. The truth is that it is the small incidents and tiny actions which have a far greater effect.

Take the Matterhorn. It was built up by tiny mica flakes. "Sand is weighty", says the Proverbs. Why? Because it is made up of millions of the minutest grains which are each one so light they wouldn't affect even the most delicate balance. Don't look upon the trivialities of life as insignificant. Every day is the child of all yesterdays.

Don't seek for the great moment rather seek to make every moment great.

July 8th

"The hand of the diligent will rule but the slothful will be put to forced labour." Proverbs 12:24

So you want to lie back and not bother. Your circumstances are ringing bells in your life and saying that it is high time you took action about certain matters that demand attention. What you don't realise is that you are arm-in-arm with the slickest old thief in the world. His whisper gets you every time. He says "there is no hurry". He is stealing incentive and blessing in your life every day. The best police force in the world couldn't apprehend him for his name is "Procrastination".

If you don't turn your back on "Procrastination" you will find that another will soon dictate the pace. His name is "Forced Labour" and he will make you do things you never dreamt you would have to do. "Too late" is the saddest phrase in human language. That you will recognise you have been a fool won't help you one bit.

Read today's proverb again and act upon it.

July 9th

"Deliver those who are drawn toward death and hold back those stumbling to the slaughter. If you say, 'Surely we did not know this', does not he who weighs the heart consider it? He who keeps your soul, does he not know it? And will he not render to each man according to his deeds?" Proverbs 24:11-12

There are more murderers in this world that the occupants of Death Row. If we neglect to save a life, when we have opportunity to, we kill it. Even governments who leave people uncared for to die have blood on their hands. Violence slays thousands but the crime of neglect slays tens of thousands.

There is no law on earth that says I must warn of the dangers of drugs, or try to save a drowning man, or give the Gospel to a perishing soul, or take time out with my children. The one who has delivered me, though is watching and he demands that I must seek to deliver others. Draw someone back from disaster, today. You can't plead ignorance to people's need. Just look around you.

July 10th

"Who has woe? Who has sorrow? Who has contentions? Who has complaints? Who has wounds without cause? Who has redness of eyes? Those who linger long at the wine." Proverbs 23:29-30

Why put an enemy in your mouth to steal away your brains? Who wants to drink that which will make you fall over and wound yourself? Who wants to swallow liquid which will cause your sight to be dimmed? Those who are lazy in their attitude to the potential of alcohol.

One day I spoke with a church elder who told me of the evening his son came home, reeling and roaring drunk. He remonstrated with him. "But Dad", he said, "you were the one who gave me my first Shandy". Selah.

July 11th

"Sand is weighty." Proverbs 27:3

What is lighter than a grain of sand? What is heavier than a bag of it? Let sand grains gather and they will crush pyramids. So it is that the accumulation of small things carries weight.

In a family, for example, communication is vital. If its members don't take time to listen to each other, to talk to each other, is it any wonder that the accumulation of such laziness ends in disaster? I know of a person who read his newspapers, watched his T.V. and never, no never, had an in-depth-conversation with his wife. One day she told him she didn't know whether she loved him any more. No wonder. It was Dostoyevsky who said "Much unhappiness has come into the world because of things left unsaid". A family that communicates makes a happy family as much as grains of sand make a lovely beach.

July 12th

"That I may cause those who love me to inherit wealth, that I may fill their treasuries." Proverbs 8:21

Warning: The following story could start something pretty amazing.

Dr. Dan Benson once walked into a chemists and asked for a box of jellatin capsules. "What for?", asked the bewildered chemist. "For a gift to my wife to put little notes in. She will open one each week for the next year", he explained. And she did. Some of them read "One good, long walk together". "One new outfit of your choice". "Two nights of freedom from dishwashing", etc. He says half the fun was watching his wife continuously fight off the urge to open them all at once. He also put in a loaded one now and again which let her claim the activity or gift during that day! It sure took any laziness out of his marriage. How about it, lads?

July 13th

"The path of the just is like the shining sun, that shines more and more unto the perfect day." Proverbs 4:18

I stood, the other day in Cary Grant's footprints. Come to think of it I tried Fred Astair's too and even Humphrey Bogart's. It was all on a sidewalk, of course, in Hollywood where famous footprints are incased in concrete.

The tinsel of Tinsel Town soon vanishes, though. The Greta Garbo's that become the Meryl Streep's that become the whoever's, are marked by impermanence. As I stood on that Hollywood sidewalk I wondered who are the truly permanent stars? It's not hard for a christian to answer that question, is it? "Those who are wise shall shine like the brightness of the firmament", says the book of Daniel, "And those who turn many to righteousness like the stars for ever and ever". Are you a star?

July 14th

"All the ways of a man are pure in his own eyes, but the Lord weighs the spirit. Commit your works to the Lord, and your thoughts will be established." Proverbs 16:2-3

We all have a lazy, blind attitude to what is wrong in ourselves and in our behaviour but we are not so lazy when it comes to judging others. Goodness, there are some folks who would let themselves be entertained by a sleazy film on T.V. and then when a minister comes on for a five minutes spiritual talk they tear him apart for not being "evangelical" enough!

Our proverb is saying that God weighs our motivations. Since we make such terrible blunders in the judgement of our own behaviour and since God makes such an accurate assessment of it, the commonsense thing to do is to put ourselves and all we do into his hands and then our motives will be refined. So, whatever you are about to do today, commit it to God before you do it. You will find such an action to be a tremendous purifier.

July 15th

"Hatred stirs up strife but love covers all sins." Proverbs 10:12

Mrs. Mullen's shortbread is my favourite. The lady from Bryansford has some special ingredient in her shortbread which makes me travel miles to eat the delectable stuff. She should patent the thing! I wonder what the special ingredient is?

In life there is one ingredient for which nothing can compensate. It is called love. When faced with misbehaviour love does not have a cast-iron severity which sees nothing but wrong. Love puts all conduct in another light. It can overlook wrongs and accept prodigals back again. It covers sin by conquering it and leads the erring person back to the practice of purity. Whatever you do, if you are lazy and leave love out, it will come to nothing.

"For surely there is a hereafter and your hope will not be cut off."
Proverbs 23:18

I passed the spot today where I stood one year ago and said good-bye to an outstanding christian gentleman called Louis Houghton. I wondered then as I looked into the face of a very sick Louis if I would ever see him again on earth. I discovered today I won't. Louis, they tell me has gone to be with Christ.

I felt sad. I missed his cheerful spirit and his Christ-likeness. He was not a lazy christian and his gentle encouragement was an inspiration. I have been wondering what he is doing now in Christ's presence. He certainly doesn't need my sermons this year. Have I lost my brother-in-Christ, Louis? No. How can you say you have lost something if you know where it is?

"The person who labours, labours for himself, for his hungry mouth draws him on." Proverbs 16:26

The need for food is the mainspring of work, so hunger is a blessing. As this is true for the body, so it is true of the soul. "Blessed are they who hunger and thirst after righeousness", said the Lord Jesus, "for they shall be filled".

Do you have a craving for righteousness and a thirst for spiritual things? Does this drive you to labour for the bread which comes down from Heaven? If so, cherish the craving and thirsting. The Bible teaches that Christ's sustenance was to do his Father's will. That is what drove him. Stop for a moment and reflect. Just what is it that drives you?

July 18th

"A tranquil heart is life to the body." Proverbs 14:30

Now I know I have been blazing away at laziness in this month's readings but let's not go overboard. We don't want to get into a lifestyle which is so hectic we feel guilty if we pause to reflect, relax, listen and learn.

Routine is the thing which speeds up life. It was Thomas Mann who said "When one day is like all the others then they are all like one; complete uniformity would make the longest life seem short and as though it has stolen away from us unawares". Familiarity with life makes time speed quickly. Why do children find time long? Because each day is a step into the unknown for them and their days are long as they gather experience.

So, take time to try new things and life will slow down.

July 19th

"Prepare your outside work, make it fit for yourself in the field; and afterward build your house." Proverbs 24:27

The best way to get something done is to begin. Charles Dickens furtively posted his first manuscript to an editor one night as a complete unknown. Even Dickens had to begin somewhere. So must you. Every great journey begins with that first step. In order to step on the moon Neill Armstrong had to first step into school as a little child. I remember crying on my first day at school but I'm not crying now as I write for you. Starting is always the hardest part of any task. So, begin, now, before something distracts you. Its half the battle. Soon you will be crossing the project off as "done".

"Does not wisdom cry out and understanding lift up her voice?"
Proverbs 8:1

The key to wisdom and understanding when dealing with our work schedules is to distinguish between what is "important" and what is "urgent". Most things marked "urgent" are simply the result of poor planning. Haven't you found that? Are all the urgent things that tug at you today really the important things?

A businessman once laid out his priorities as;
1. My relationship with God.
2. My relationship with my wife.
3. My relationship with my children.
4. My personal development.
5. My business.

Wisdom, indeed.

July 21st

"By sorrow of the heart the spirit is broken." Proverbs 15:13

How you think when you lose determines how long it will be until you win. That's a fact. All of us have disappointments, sometimes crushing ones but we must not get lazy and give up. "From unseen origins and clay there grows so ugly roots and thorns and then, the rose". Every major character in the Bible you can think of had overwhelming disappointments in their lives. Sometimes their biggest disappointment was themselves. Yet, they yielded to God and he made their lives beautiful. Are you losing? Yield to God. He will heal your broken heart and spirit.

July 22nd

"Do you see a man who excels in his work? He will stand before kings; he will not stand before unknown men." Proverbs 22:29

Does your work loom so large and difficult in front of you that you want to run away from it? We have already written that the most important part of attempting a project is to begin. The next most important part is to take it in stages. Always remember that Nehemiah first took his project to his heart, then he took it to the Lord and then he took it to the people. The wall of Jerusalem was rebuilt in stages. Let's put it this way; by the mile it's a trial; by the yard it's hard; by the inch it's a cinch. Go to it and remember today's proverb is one of God's mighty promises.

July 23rd

"Do not remove the ancient landmark." Proverbs 23:10

"Shallow men believe in luck; wise and strong men believe in cause and effect", said Emerson. No truer words were ever spoken. They also apply to today's proverb. If we rise up in our generation and lazily, without much thought, pull down the things that have stood the test of time the effect will be devastating. Our generation has already seen it, especially in family life.

100 years ago the Sunday sermon from the Bible was the chief means of instruction now millions despise the Bible. Look at the result in the areas of authority and integrity in our nation. Abortion, homosexuality, divorce, crime, indiscipline, and violence are rife on an unprecedented scale. Before you decide to remove something long cherished from your life, think long about the effect your action will have.

"In all labour there is profit but idle chatter leads only to poverty."
Proverbs 14:23

I went to school with a chap called John McCammon. He became a very successful dentist and discovered with his colleague, one day, that there was a way of removing a needle from a syringe without touching it by hand. They patented their discovery and its success has gone worldwide. Lives will be saved as a result.

Duane Pearsall was testing a device that controls static electricity when he noticed that the smoke from a technician's cigarette caused the meter in the device to go bad. He was annoyed that he had to get a new meter installed. Later he realised that the reaction of the meter to smoke might prove valuable. He invented the first American made smoke detector alarm system!

Frequently golden opportunities in life are right under our noses while we idle away our time with chatter. Don't be lazy. Get in the habit of looking for them. That's wisdom.

"The hope of the righteous is gladness." *Proverbs 10:28*

If you brood over your troubles you will have a perfect hatch. What good does your brooding do? None. Those little birds in the air around you; do they have problems? They certainly do. They face inclement weather, have their homes wrecked, their eggs taken, and predators hound them most of their days. Yet, their brooding is not like ours. They are without anxious care. Consider them. Why should a little bird be glad and its life span so short when you, christian, who will be with Christ for ever, go around with your stomach behaving like a spin dryer? Face your problems. Work by all means but don't worry. The hope of the righteous is gladness.

July 26th

"The fear of man brings a snare but he who trusts in the Lord will be exalted." Proverbs 29:25

Who cares who gets the credit as long as the Lord gets the glory? So many people live unimaginative, unadventurous lives because they didn't get credit for what they did in the past and pull back from the good projects in which they were involved because people didn't recognise their worth.

A christian need never have that hang-up. Why? Because the Lord recognises their worth. They should walk in the conscious knowledge that they are beloved of the Lord. They should do everything to His glory and not care two hoots whether people give them credit for what they are doing. If God gets the glory isn't that what really matters? So, onward!

July 27th

"Better is a little with the fear of the Lord, than great treasure with trouble." Proverbs 15:16

The average person's vocabulary is about 500 words. That's a fascinating statistic, isn't it? Yet, look what a Mark Twain or a Shakespeare did with that vocabulary. There are not actually many basic colours but Michael Angelo didn't feel restricted, did he? There are only 7 basic notes but Beethoven or Charles Wesley, Chopin or Graham Kendrick didn't find them too few to start developing their classics, did they?

Don't ever complain that your circumstances are too restricting. You don't need much in order to do much. In the final analysis a little is better with the fear of the Lord than great treasure and trouble with it.

July 28th

"For three things the earth is perturbed, yes, for four it cannot bear up: For a servant when he reigns, a fool when he is filled with food, a hateful woman when she is married, and a maidservant who succeeds her mistress." Proverbs 30:21-23

I have been thinking particularly of the last little statement in this fascinating series of four proverbs. It speaks of a maidservant who succeeds her mistress and how everyone is worried as to whether or not she might be lazy or inept or perhaps throw her weight around. It reminds me of the story someone once told. He said, "My grandmother rode in a horse and carriage but she was afraid to ride in a car. My mother rode in a car, but she was afraid to ride on a plane. I ride in a plane but I am afraid to ride in a jet. My daughter rides in a jet, but is afraid to ride in a horse and carriage!" All progress, in fact, is invariably followed by regress. Let's watch this subtle inverted laziness in our generation that ignores the progress that our forebears have made.

July 29th

"Every purpose is established by counsel." Proverbs 20:18

At school they always told me that anything worth doing was worth doing well. Yet, a revised version of that would surely be that anything worth doing is worth doing poorly! If you set out to do something well your initial attempt may prove that you are not very good at it. Yet, as you learn new skills and techniques you will get better and soon you will be doing your project very well.

I have often heard young folk pray in public for the first time. They may stumble out a few words and appear pretty hopeless. I have watched someone attempt to witness for the Lord and not be very good at adapting themselves to people's needs. Yet, with God's help and quiet persistence some of those people have become great public servants of God and some have gone on to be the greatest witnesses of their generation. Attempt things and even though you may at first do them poorly with good counsel, courage and the fear of the Lord you will improve. You wouldn't want to end up like the man of whom it was said that in his life he had "No hits, no runs, no errors".

July 30th

"The way of the slothful man is like a hedge of thorns, but the way of the upright is a highway." Proverbs 15:19

How important are externals to you? I want you to answer these following questions, honestly. Do you judge a person by; (a) their choice of clothes? (b) their weight? (c) their length of hair? (d) the address where they live? (e) their standard of education? (f) their colour? (g) their job? (h) their financial position? (i) their denominational affiliation?

To put it simply; do you think you would have gone to hear John the Baptist? He might have looked lazy but of those born of woman there has never been a greater. His path was, in fact, a highway. Look beyond the externals.

"As a door turns on its hinges, so does the slothful turn on his bed."
Proverbs 26:14

Some folk wouldn't even get out of bed to encourage someone else. How lazy we often are in encouraging one another! Do you realise that you can make someone's day by simply being kind to them? I love the story of the lady who was taken to dinner by William Gladstone, the distinguished British Prime Minister. The next evening she attended a dinner where she sat next to Benjamin Disraeli, his equally distinguished opponent. When someone asked her what she thought of the two men she replied, "After sitting with Mr. Gladstone I was convinced he was the cleverest man in England but after sitting next to Mr. Disraeli I though I was the cleverest woman in England!" Go on, don't be lazy!

AUGUST

It's a holiday month in the Western world, a time for making new friends and renewing acquaintances with those of longstanding. It's time for a chat over the garden fence (or the swimming pool!) with a neighbour or two; a barbecue on the lawn, a picnic on the beach. Friends and neighbours is our topic from the Book of Proverbs this month. Let the insight Solomon gives become a deep enrichment of this important area of our lives.

August 1st

"Do not withhold good from those to whom it is due when it is in the power of your hand to do so. Do not say to your neighbour, 'Go and come back and tomorrow I will give it', when you have it with you." Proverbs 3:27-28

I recently read about a man who writes down the name of every person he has met. He is now 83 and he has written down the name of everyone he has met, that he can remember, since he was 3 years old! He has 3,487 people in his yellow binder! You may meet a lot of people or just one person today and if it is within the power of your hand to do them good, do so. Do you owe your neighbour money? ; please remember that the money you owe is not yours. To use it for your own purposes is dishonest. Do good to your new acquaintances and pay your bills to your old ones; today. When F. B. Meyer preached one night on 'Holiness' at the Keswick Convention the local Post Office ran out of postal orders the next day because so many christians were paying their bills after hearing Meyer's message from God's word. Selah.

"Do not devise evil against your neighbour for he dwells by you for safety sake. Do not strive with a man without a cause if he has done you no harm." Proverbs 3:29-30

Our first proverb today is about the abuse of confidence. The meaning of the first expression has to do with "ploughing evil" against your neighbour. It is used in the sense of a ploughman preparing the land for sowing. To purposely plan to do your neighbour harm when he has confidence in you means that your neighbour has misplaced his confidence and you are in trouble when your sin finds you out. Don't "plough evil" against your neighbour or you will reap a frightening harvest.

The meaning of the second paragraph is clear; do not strive or quarrel with the person who has given you no offence. Brer Rabbit's Tar Baby got him into endless trouble, didn't he? So, don't plot evil against your neighbour and don't cause trouble with people who mean no trouble.

August 3rd

"My son if you become surety for your friend, if you have shaken hands in pledge for a stranger, you are snared by the words of your own mouth; you are taken by the words of your mouth. So do this, my son, and deliver yourself; for you have come to the hand of your friend; go and humble yourself; plead with your friend. Give no sleep to your eyes, nor slumber to your eyelids. Deliver yourself like a gazelle from the hand of the hunter, and like a bird from the hand of the fowler." Proverbs 6:1-5

What a warning! Going "guarantor" is a dangerous business. It could mean that you might lose everything. Have you been snared into it by a hasty word or action? By hook or by crook get out of hampering yourself by imposed obligation even if it means humbling yourself and confessing that you have undertaken more than righteousness and foresight would advise.

August 4th

"A ... neighbour's wife, whoever touches her will not go unpunished." Proverbs 6:27-29

How can I tell who will read these words? I leave you with Dr. Harry Ironside's comment on this frightening proverb about an adulterer. He said; "How many a dreadful blot upon an otherwise upright and honoured life has resulted from what at first was a thoughtless familiarity which led on step by step to the awful overthrow of uprightness and virtue, culminating in lifelong sorrow. No other sin, unless it be the taking of human life which is often its fearful result, leaves so dreadful a stain behind, as with David's case". Selah.

August 5th

"The hypocrite with his mouth destroys his neighbour but through knowledge the right will be delivered." Proverbs 11:9

Potiphar's wife certainly set out to destroy her neighbour, Joseph. Hypocrites usually cover up their sins by slandering their neighbour. It is interesting to remember that it was God who through history vindicated Joseph and he suffered long because of a hypocrite during his lifetime.

It could be that some hypocrite has ruined your life and reputation, or, is trying to. Don't be discouraged, the proverb promises that "through knowledge the righteous will be delivered". God knows all about your innocence and sooner or later the truth will come out. Nothing is surer. How does Potiphar's wife stand now?

August 6th

"He who is devoid of wisdom despises his neighbour but a man of understanding holds his peace." Proverbs 11:12

Don't sneer at your fellow citizens! Don't use words of contempt against your neighbour! An understanding person is slow to condemn and makes allowance for others difficulties. If people of understanding cannot approve of what their neighbour does at least they know how to be silent. A person of sense keeps quiet. "Do not let your mouth lead you into sin", warns Solomon in Ecclesiastes 5:6. So many sins begin with words and it would be a dreadful business if your words led you to sin with respect to your neighbours. You have got to live beside them whether you like it or not. Don't make things worse. Hold your peace!

August 7th

"The righteous should chose his friends carefully, for the way of the wicked leads them astray." Proverbs 12:26

When I was at school I remember reading Dean Swift's "Gulliver's Travels" and reading how Gulliver got so fed up with human beings that he went and talked to horses because he found them more amenable! In my youthful mind I thought Swift very extreme in his view of human nature. I understand now, all too well, what he was driving at!

Be careful who you let close to your heart. Watch who you let influence your decision making processes. Guard against those who come too close to your "dreams". Chose your friends carefully for there are people once they come close to you will try to lay yokes on your back that will bear you down and ruin you. Christ's yoke is easy and his burden is light. Other yokes will lead you astray.

August 8th

"The poor man is hated even by his own neighbour but the rich has many friends. He who despises his neighbour sins but he who has mercy on the poor, happy is he." Proverbs 14:20-21

Few are the people who talk about their poor relatives! Poverty is certainly an object of dislike and riches draw goodwill like a magnet. In this world covetousness often rules and the rich will always have people to praise them. Let us then be very careful never to look down upon, or despise the poverty of anyone, whether they be friend or neighbour. Compassion for those who are in trouble is a divine feeling. It carries God's approval. So, don't laud the rich and don't despise the poor. Stay balanced.

August 9th

"A friend loves at all times and a brother is born for adversity." Proverbs 17:17-18

Here is the portrait of a true friend. The word "friend" is used loosely in life and it is good to re-define its true qualities. According to our proverb the essential note of true friendship is unvariable affection. That doesn't mean that the true friend always bubbles in a display of affection for their friend but rather that as still waters run deep, so their friendship is steady.

True friendship is independent of time. It does not wear out with years. It is independent of circumstances. It survives poverty or riches. True friendship isn't shaken by slander, outlives shabby treatment and isn't just shown when adversity comes.

Your brother will turn up when you are in trouble but a friend is there good times and bad. How do you measure up, friend?

August 10th

"The first one to plead his cause seems right until his neighbour comes and examines him." Proverbs 18:17

There are two sides to everything. Before you judge something it is vital that you hear the other side. No matter who tells you his side of the story he cannot give you absolute accuracy. He may intentionally misrepresent it or unconsciously mis-state it. This is particularly true when you are trying to help someone whose marriage is in trouble. You tend to believe the first partner who comes to you.

You owe it to the complainant, to the defendant, to yourself and to the cause of Christ, to hear both sides. Its harder work but it brings greater reward.

August 11th

"A man who has friends must himself be friendly." Proverbs 18:24

It is reputed that a famous British politician, many years ago met a fellow MP on the steps of the House of Commons and asked him for the loan of sixpence to ring a friend. His colleague, with a sparkle in his eye, said, "Here's a shilling ring all your friends!"

I hope you are not so badly off for friends! Yet, I wonder, if someone reading today's proverb has a hard time making friends. If so, turn the searchlight of this lovely proverb upon your life. If you want friends, you had better start saying "Hello" and "How are you" and "How does your garden grow?" Perhaps you could try what the one and only Matthew Boland tried one day. Matthew was an evangelist here in Northern Ireland and he said to a mechanic who was working under a car, one day, "Would you like a Polo mint?" The mechanic was very anti-christian and Matthew was trying to get him to attend some evangelistic services. How could you refuse a man with a 'friendly' Polo mint? He didn't, went to the services, became a christian and, eventually, a Presbyterian minister!

August 12th

"There is a friend that sticketh closer than a brother."
Proverbs 18:24

You may have many people, both bad and good alike who will feed off you, exhaust your resources and when trouble comes, won't stand by you. Don't think that it is the number of friends you have that is the really useful thing in your life. There is amongst your friends that particular friend who sticks with you through thick and thin. Treasure him or her. Closer even than a brother, more loyal, more compassionate. Never take that friend for granted.

Christians know that Christ's love will never desert them and that his love too is closer than any relatives. Walk in the conscious knowledge that you are beloved of the Lord. In my experience I have found people who give me the distinct impression that they think I am not beloved of the Lord. Why should I let them intimidate me? Why should you? They wouldn't die for us, would they? He did.

August 13th

"Wealth makes many friends but the poor is separated from his friend." Proverbs 19:4

Think of the prodigal son. Those girls he knew cared only for his money, didn't they? They were fickle friends. If you have some time on your hands today sit down and read through the parable that follows the story of the prodigal son. It occurs in Luke chapter 16 and concerns a man who used the resources he had to gain for himself some friends who would remain his friends when his resources were gone for ever.

The Lord Jesus taught in the parable that those who follow him should use the "mammon" of unrighteousness (personal possessions) to make eternal friends. How? Well, if, for example, you used your spare cash to, say, send a Gideon Bible somewhere and someone got converted to Christ through it do you not think that person would be glad to see you in Heaven? You would have a friend for ever.

Wealth may make a person a lot of friends on earth but using what you have for the cause of Christ will make you friends that will last for ever.

Some people will have more friends in Heaven than others. Selah.

August 14th

"Debate your case with your neighbour himself and do not disclose the secret to another; lest he who hears it expose your shame and your reputation be ruined." Proverbs 25:9-10

If you have a controversy with your neighbour, deal with him, privately, in a friendly way. Don't bring in any secret given to you by another to support your cause. If you are found out you will find your reputation ruined.

If someone says to you "Please don't tell anyone what I am about to tell you", prove that you can be trusted. Remember, not only is the secret at stake but so is your reputation if you agree to keep it.

It was Solomon who originated the saying that "a little bird told me". Don't join the species because they frequently get shot down and are never heard of again.

August 15th

"Seldom set foot in your neighbour's house; lest he become weary of you and hate you." Proverbs 25:17

I once went to hear the famous writer and broadcaster David Kossoff tell Bible stories in a school hall. The crowd, including me, clapped and clapped asking for an encore. He came out and told us about his father who was a Jewish-Russian tailor who came to London. He explained how that his father had taught him a principle which he put very succinctly to his son. "One night", he said to David, "you will be in a home and the conversation will be rich and the chemistry between you and the people will be good. Always remember whenever that happens, don't stay too long". With that Kossoff walked off that stage and I have never seen him in the flesh since.

What the old tailor advised also applies to visits to your neighbours. Not only make them reasonably short, make them reasonably infrequent, or else.

"Do not be a witness against your neighbour without cause for would you deceive with your lips? Do not say 'I will do to him just as he has done to me; I will render to the man according to his work'". Proverbs 24:28-29

If your neighbour has done you wrong don't set out to ruin him with revenge in your heart. Anyway, if you are always trying to defend your name at every turn, even with your neighbour, you will be busy. Leave the defence of your name with God. When you sling mud back you are the one who is losing ground!

The proverb, of course, does qualify such non-retalitory behaviour. It says you must not witness against your neighbour "without cause". This means that we must not mention our neighbour's faults, unless for some very good reason, and, certainly never for malice or for love of gossip. Whatever you do keep revenge out of your heart because it will destroy you, not your neighbour.

August 17th

"Like a mad man who throws firebrands, arrows and death, is the man who deceives his neighbour and says 'I was only joking'." Proverbs 26:18-19

Firebrands are darts with blazing material attached to them. Think of how lethal they are in the hands of someone who is deranged who throws them about recklessly and indiscriminately. He could easily kill someone. So is the person who deceives his neighbour and then says "I was only joking".

If someone hurts his neighbour with lies, the plea that he was only joking is not allowed. No amount of flannel about "it was not done seriously" will cover the damage done. As insane people ill treat their doctors and nurses so are those who injure friends in secret and then try to excuse themselves, when discovered, by insisting they were only joking. So, be careful.

August 18th

"The north wind brings forth rain and a backbiting tongue an angry countenance." Proverbs 25:23

There is a time to smile and a time to frown. If a person doesn't have the faculty of frowning I wouldn't give much for his smile, would you? Let's love good and hate evil. Salt is useless if it loses its saltness and let's not forget that the Saviour said "Have salt in yourselves and have peace with one another".

When a backbiting tongue enters the community of friends and neighbours it would be harmless if it never met with itching ears. It would be like seed without soil or a spark without tinder. So let's knit our brows at the start of the backbiter's speel. Like a medicine you don't need to harbour lots of it in large quanities everywhere you go but a tincture within reach at all times is very useful. Keep your frowns handy and administer liberally to the backbiter.

August 19th

"As iron sharpens iron, so a man sharpens the countenance of his friend." Proverbs 27:17

When an iron tool becomes blunt an instrument of the same material is sometimes used to restore its edge. Iron literally sharpens iron.

Have you known sorrow and care in your life? Then you will know how they blunt your spirit and take the edge off living. Yet, bring a downcast person into the presence of a true friend who sparkles with hope and encouragement and slowly the blunted mind takes on a new edge and is able again to cut through even seemingly overwhelming difficulties. Human sympathy is a very powerful force. Even the embattled Paul pled with young Timothy to come and see him in prison; a cheerful face and a word of cheer will beat a lot of tracts and theological books sent in the post any day; agreed?

August 20th

"The wicked flee when no one pursues but the righteous are as bold as a lion." Proverbs 28:1

You remember Cain. He would not have been a good neighbour to know or a good relative either. It is interesting to note that when he killed Abel, no one pursued him and yet he was certainly pursued. He said "I shall be a fugitive and a vagabond on the earth and it will happen that anyone who finds me will kill me". It was almost as though every leaf that moved made him jump. Conscience is a fierce pursurer.

No matter how fast you run you will never be able to run away from yourself. If you get right with God, in Christ you need fear nothing, not even those skeletons in your cupboard. "The blood of Jesus Christ his Son cleanses us from all sin". Rest in its power and it will make you as bold as a lion and a good friend to know.

August 21st

"A poor man is better than a liar." Proverbs 19:22

All around you are cheats. They cheat their friends and their neighbours. They cheat the law and the government. They even cheat themselves. They call evil good and good evil. Always remember that no matter how high flying an individaul might be people always call a dishonest person a liar. No matter how poor a person may be, if he or she is honest they can lift up their head and look folks straight in the eye.

Don't you think this proverb is an excellent motto for anyone, anywhere, who is involved in business? Put it on your desk, or even better, in your heart. It is a short and simple legend. "A poor man is better than a liar".

August 22nd

"All the ways of a man are pure in his own eyes but the Lord weighs the spirits. Commit your works to the Lord and your thoughts will be established." Proverbs 16:2

This proverb is teaching that there is an amazing power of self deception in a human heart. People like the things they do and do the things that they like. Sadly while they do things that are pure in their own eyes they forget that other eyes are watching and weighing their actions in his balance.

How can I weigh my actions amongst my neighbours and friends in the community so that they will pass the scrutiny of God's balance? The answer is I must commit my actions to the Lord, first. The Hebrew means "roll it over on Jehovah". Test it with him then your thoughts will be established. It's a promise.

185

August 23rd

"A scoffer seeks wisdom and does not find it but knowledge is easy to him who understands." Proverbs 14:6

Secularism is the Latin for "this-world-ism". It means "attend to the world you are now in". Few of us are not tempted by its subtleties. It is particularly powerful when applied to our schools and in turn affects our communities. The great trend is to train children in secular knowledge and to leave the Bible and its absolutes out.

It is a shame when the Scriptures are left out of a child's education because they have influenced the conduct and history of mankind more than all books put together. Let a garden choose of its own accord what it will grow and it will grow weeds. Let a child choose and it will choose sin. Christians are not seeking ultimate truth, they have found it. That truth gives them an understanding in all the knowledge that they come across in life. To deny a child such truth would be a tragedy. Let's teach it.

August 24th

"The mouth of the righteous is the well of life ... wise people store up knowledge." Proverbs 10:11-14

The wicked are like the troubled sea. They are restless and throw up spray that destroys every green thing within reach. Sin propagates sin. Ungodly people often corrupt their neighbours and unsuspecting young people also get caught. The righteous have the very opposite affect.

Wise people store up wisdom and they don't put their winnings into a bag with holes, either. They turn everything to good account. Losses are converted into gain. Even faults that they have commited and that make them blush now, may be turned into a very valuable source of wisdom. Don't let anything in your life trickle away. The dearer it is the more useful it will be. It is a tragedy if you are always paying and never possessing. Remember that the cleverest people are often the least successful. One godly person may hold more than the world's balances are able to weigh.

August 25th

"The generous soul will be made rich and he who waters will also be watered himself." Proverbs 11:25

There is a law in space, is there not? The earth affects the moon and the moon affects the earth; each planet influences all the others. Remove one and you disturb the order of the rest.

So it is in life. One person's behaviour affects the rest either for good or evil. A stream seems to sink without trace into the sea but actually rises later in evaporation and falls on us in refreshing rain or dew. Our proverb applies this principle to our lives. If I reach out and refresh someone's life I in turn will be refreshed. Tell me, are you a waterer or a witherer?

August 26th

"Faithful are the wounds of a friend but the kisses of an enemy are deceitful." Proverbs 27:6

Was there ever a kiss so deceitful as the man who kissed the Saviour of the world? What an incredible traitor he was. If you had seen Judas give Christ a kiss of greeting you would have thought him a friend of the greatest friend a sinner ever had. His lavish greeting was only lavish in order to hide his traitor's heart.

Beware of kisses. Nothing can be more deceitful. The wounds which a real friend may inflict on you by a just rebuke are guided by truth. "Let the righeous strike me", wrote David, "it shall be a kindness. And let him reprove me; it shall be as excellent oil; let my head not refuse it". (Psalm 141:5). Heed this advice.

August 27th

"A man who flatters his neighbour is spreading a net for his steps."
Proverbs 29:5

I always remember when James Galway, the flautist, was interviewed in hospital in Geneva after he had suffered an unfortunate accident he commented that the accident had actually done him good because it had given him time to reflect. He said his problem at that time in his life had been that he was beginning to believe what the posters were saying about him. His brush with death had sobered and re-directed him. If you are only saying what is agreeable to your neighbour and applauding his every word and his lifestyle indiscriminately, he may begin to believe you and be self-deceived: you would be spreading a net for his steps. Beware of the flatterer.

August 28th

"He who blesses his friend with a loud voice, rising early in the morning, it will be counted a curse to him." *Proverbs 27:14*

Insincerity is a miserable thing. Here is someone who is pouring out praises to his friend "early in the morning". What is the proverb driving at when it notes that he does it so early in the day? It is highlighting that the insincere person is tactless and doesn't wait for a convenient moment to express how he feels. Timing is the thing and ill timing can bring insincerity to light. The flatterer is hoping for future benefits. The person on the receiving end would just as soon be cursed by him as blessed. "He who loudly scolds, praises; and he who excessively praises, scolds. They are not believed because they exaggerate", said Luther. Too right.

August 29th

"Better is a neighbour nearby than a brother far away."
Proverbs 27:9

Don't you think that friendship is founded upon sympathy? Your relatives may or may not be sympathetic to you. The true friend, though, has been trusted and tried in all sorts of circumstances through your life and can be thoroughly depended upon. Notice that the words "nearby" and "far away" in our proverb can refer to feeling just as much as locality.

The proverb is saying that we would be wise to truly appreciate those who are near to us. Let's cultivate our neighbour by a kind action today.

August 30th

"Better is a dry morsel with quietness than a house full of feasting with strife." Proverbs 17:1

If the people in a family or community care for each other and love each other they don't need to have great riches to enjoy an excellent quality of life. Your table could be loaded with food but envy, strife and jealousy be rampant amongst your guests or family and your meal be miserable. The Bible proverb does not imply that all happy families or communities eat dry morsels nor is it saying that all rich families or communities do not know love. It is saying that riches can't secure happiness and poverty can't destroy it. If you know love, and especially God's love, you will be happy even in the hard times, if you don't, you will be miersable even in times of material prosperity.

August 31st

"Whoever trusts in the Lord shall be safe." Proverbs 29:25

Today I have been in the Southernmost town on the face of the earth. Next stop, as the albatross flies, is the South Pole. My friends Mr. and Mrs. Melhop, took me to Bluff harbour and I watched a huge ship being manoeuvred out into the winter seas. The straits it entered are amongst the most dangerous in the world.

As I saw the huge vessel move out towards the horizon I noticed the little pilot boat bringing the pilot back into harbour again. "Fortunately", said a lady, "the pilot doesn't have to go any further." Immediately I thought of my Saviour who came aboard the vessel of my life when I was a little boy and in all of these years he has never left me. When Christ comes on board the vessel of anyones life he does not leave when the ship heads into the gales of winter or sails in the calm waters of summer. He has promised never to leave nor forsake us. He will bring all who trust in him safely to that heavenly harbour. As your friends and neighbours see your confidence in him may they bid him come on board the vessels of their lives, too. They will not be sorry.

SEPTEMBER

I am always intigued with the little word "but". You know, everything was going smoothly "but ...". It was a pleasant conversation "but ...". You had an excellent holiday "but ...". He is a decent enough fellow "but ...". The local church is a place of great fellowship "but ...".

All over the book of Proverbs you will find that the little word "but" is employed to link contrasts. As summer slips away from us let's get into the contrasts of Proverbs; they are intriguing and filled with promise.

September 1st

"Those who are of a perverse heart are an abomination to the Lord, but, such as are blameless in their ways are His delight."
Proverbs 11:20

A little boy got knocked down once by a man who was rushing to catch a train. The child had had a jigsaw in his hand and the pieces were now scattered all over the pavement. Feeling sorry for what he had done, the man got down on his knees and began to pick up the pieces. People had trampled all over the jigsaw pieces as they rushed by, but, despite the pressure, he kept up his good work and managed to retrieve them. As the crowd surged on, the man straightened up to hear the little boy ask him a question.

"Sir", asked the child, "is your name, Jesus?"

September 2nd

"The sacrifice of the wicked is an abomination to the Lord but the prayer of the upright is His delight." Proverbs 15:8

Tell me, would you delight in someone requesting something of you who was in reality a rank hypocrite and who had neither love nor respect for you? Would you delight in a sweet talking person who led a double life? You would abhor such hypocrisy, wouldn't you? So does God.

I find the words of God to his people Israel in the book of Isaiah most moving. "When you come to appear before me", says God, "who has required this from your hand, to trample my courts? Bring no more futile sacrifices incense is an abomination to me. The New Moons, the Sabbaths, and the calling of assemblies - I cannot endure iniquity and the sacred meeting. Your New Moons and your appointed feasts my soul hates; they are a trouble to me, I am weary of bearing them ... even though you make many prayers I will not hear". What would you contrast with such hypocrisy? Today's proverb will give you the answer. Which category do you and I fall into?

September 3rd

"The hope of the righteous will be gladness but the expectation of the wicked will perish." Proverbs 10:28

"Promises", says the man of the world, "that's all you christians live on; future promises". We simply want to ask what life would be like without promises. Examine your heart and you will agree that desires are an essential part of our human personality. Milk bottles don't have desires. They will stay where you put them. Humans are not content with the immediate it is the future that they hope for. You are nearly dead if you don't have any desires; pity the man or woman who has no desires left. The thing is, what are you going to focus your desires on?

If you focus your desires on the wrong things they will give you enjoyment but they will progressively enslave you until you get into a morass of an eternity without God. Centre your desires on Christ and His word and His promises will not disappoint you. Christian hope is not "hope so."

September 4th

"When the righteous are in authority, the people rejoice; but when a wicked man rules, the people groan." Proverbs 29:2

Does the Gospel leave the area of politics untouched? Certainly not. Commercial life, literature, art, recreation, society and politics all come under the influence of the Gospel. The welfare of any people is determined by the moral character of its government. A country gets the government it wants. If the people won't have it, it will crash, eventually. Europe in the 90's has certainly proved that. So, if you want to influence the government, influence the people. If you want to influence the people, preach and teach the Gospel and who can tell what position of responsibility the people it influences will find themselves in? Good people will make good laws. Sow good seed, everywhere. The results are often nationwide.

September 5th

"By transgression an evil man is snared, but the righteous sings and rejoices." Proverbs 29:6

To see an animal snared is a pathetic sight. There is no way of escape, unless someone sets it free. To see people snared by sin is even more pathetic. Only the Lord Jesus can set them free and many of them, when he approaches, think he will do them more harm than the sin that grips them! They actually resist release.

Is someone reading these lines, today, and you are snared by some sin? The Lord Jesus is totally qualified to be the sinner's Saviour, turn to Him now and let Him release you. The result will be a release that will bring total forgiveness and, whats more, will put a song in your heart. It sure beats staying in a snare. Come on out!

September 6th

"Good understanding gains favour but the way of the unfaithful is hard." Proverbs 13:15

Why do good things always seem to happen to bad people? Why do the transgressors flourish and the innocent suffer? Why do the drug and porn kings of this world who make fortunes out of people who are weak, flourish, and escape detection? Perpetrators of fraud and exploitation are everywhere and the earth doesn't swallow them up. How can the way of the transgressor, then, be hard when they seem to be having a great time?

The answer is, of course, that from the standpoint of eternity the way of the unfaithful is a disaster. They do not know the peace of God or the confidence of faith. They are limited to the pleasures their years on earth can give them. Don't envy them.

September 7th

"The integrity of the upright will guide them, but the falseness of the treacherous will destroy them." Proverbs 11:3

There is no more difficult subject than guidance. We can often see that we have been guided up to this particular point in our lives but where to go next is often the problem. As a child I learned a little poem which hung in our home on a little brass plaque illustrated by a great sailing ship at sea. It has always been an inspiration to me when choosing which direction to take in life. The poem read "One ship drives East and another drives West with the self same winds that blow, but, it is the set of the sails and not the gales that tell us the way to go".

It is a persons honesty that helps them to make the right decisions. It is a persons fear of the Lord that moves them away from falseness and treachery. What a person is determines what a person does. So, set your sails today by God's Word and it won't matter what direction the wind comes from.

September 8th

"The backslider in heart will be filled with his own ways but a good man will be satisfied from above." Proverbs 14:14

Tempted to turn away from the God you love? Tempted to throw-in-the-towel and quit? Tempted to think that the christian way is, after all, too narrow and that the seemingly broader horizons beyond the truth of God's Word are the things to chase?

Don't be fooled; behind every effect is a cause. The backslider will reap the fruit of backsliding. Our proverb says he will be filled with his own ways. What could ultimately be more miserable? Solomon later taught that everything under the sun was vanity. Too right. Better to be like the good man in our proverb who will be satisfied with the things from above the sun. Keep going on for the Lord.

"The way of the slothful man is like a hedge of thorns, but the way of the upright is a highway." Proverbs 15:19

Let's apply today's proverb to the use of the mind. We often say we have not loved the Lord our God with all our hearts, but, have we realised that we are also commanded to love Him with all our mind? We are often slothful when it comes to thinking about spiritual things never to speak about most things. Not to think is a sin. In fact, when you think about it, the essence of worry is a failure to think.

In the Scriptures man is rebuked by God when he fails to do by his mind what animals do by instinct. "Even the stork in the heavens knows her appointed time; and the turtle dove, the swift and the swallow observe the time of their coming but my people do not know the judgement of the Lord", says the Bible. Your mind matters, in worship, in evangelism, in pastoral care, in business, in raising children, in everything. Use it. Be transformed by the renewing of your mind.

"There is a way that seems right to a man, but its end is the way of death." Proverbs 14:12

Passion and self will are blinding. They make a person think their way is best. "Let conscience be your guide" is a fair enough point but conscience needs to be informed by God's Word, the Bible, in order to make it a safe guide.

Abel thought he was right, guided by blinding anger. Esau thought he was right, guided by blinding hunger. Saul thought he was right, guided by blinding jealousy. Samson thought he was right, guided by blinding lust. Jezebel thought she was right, guided by blinding pride. Belshazzar thought he was right, guided by blinding partying. But they were all wrong. Things are not always as they seem. Beware.

September 11th

"There is gold and a multitude of rubies but the lips of knowledge are a precious jewel." Proverbs 20:15

We all know that moment in life when someone says something to us that suddenly throws the light of wisdom on a problem which has long troubled us. We could almost hug them for it. Money couldn't buy such a word which can literally bring a complete change of direction in our lives.

A headmaster of a school in which I taught, once said to me, "Bingham, have you ever thought of the christian ministry?" "Why, sir", I replied "is there anything wrong with my work?" "No", he quickly replied "But it seems to me that the christian ministry is the bent of your whole life". Six months later I was giving all of my time to teaching, writing and preaching the Scriptures. He'll never know what that simple word of encouragement did for me. Use an encouraging word to someone today.

September 12th

"The Lord will destroy the house of the proud but he will establish the boundary of the widow." Proverbs 15:25

God has a very special place for widows. Again and again in Old Testament Scripture they are mentioned and laws are given for their protection. Our Proverb tells us that the proud, self confident man and his family will be rooted up but the widow in all her vulnerability and lack of protection will have special protection from the Lord.

In Old Testament times property was defined by landmarks, particularly stone landmarks and nothing was easier than to remove these or to alter them. It was a common form of fraud to do so. The Lord will move to protect the widow and special blessings attend those who do the same. Their greatest human champion in New Testament days was Luke; he writes more about them than any other writer. No wonder he was called the "beloved physician". If you are a widow may this lovely proverb encourage your lonely heart today. God has not forgotten you.

September 13th

"A man's pride will bring him low but the humble in spirit will retain honour." Proverbs 29:23

The thing which brings a man furthest down is that man's effort to exalt himself. The law of gravitation says that the higher matter shoots up, the deeper it will fall and probably be broken in the process. Don't you think the same law operates in the realm of man's spirit?

I find that there is so little recognition of God's supremacy, even in every day life, that if you say to someone when leaving them "God bless", they think you are an endangered species! Let us really seek, throughout today, to give God the glory in everything. Jealously guard God's glory in everything you say. The way of humility conducts you to safety. Remember that.

"The merciful man does good for his own soul but he who is cruel troubles his own flesh. The wicked man does deceptive work but to him who sows righteousness will be a sure reward."
Proverbs 11:17,18

Want to do yourself some good? Be merciful. When you show mercy two people benefit; you and the person in need of it. Both get good but you get the larger share because it is more blessed to give than to receive. The "but" in our proverb introduces us to a very different reward. Just as mercy reaps blessings, cruelty brings torment to both the one who inflicts it and the inflicted. You cannot hurt a person without hurting yourself. Our proverb tells us to sow righteousness and the reward is sure. Who was the only righteous one? Our Lord Jesus. He sowed in tears and his reward is and will be incalculable. Follow in His steps. It is a day lost that does not see a righteous seed sown. Will your day be lost? See that it isn't.

September 15th

"The memory of the righteous is blessed but the name of the wicked will rot." Proverbs 10:7

It is a chilling thought that comes when we consider what people will remember us for. I visited the famous Gold Trail of Octago in New Zealand's South Island, yesterday. I was given a shovel and a gold pan and set to work. The amazing thing was I found a fleck of pure gold in the black sand at the bottom of my gold pan after some intensive digging. The graveyard in this district bears witness to many who in the gold rush here in the 1860's gave their lives in quest of gold. They were frequently disillusioned.

Will you be remembered for mere money making or for the fragrance of Christ in your life? Will you be remembered for kindness or selfishness? To put it bluntly, whoever thinks of calling a child Judas or Nero? Go for the gold which does not perish.

September 16th

"Without counsel, plans go awry but in the multitude of counsellors they are established." Proverbs 15:22

Many a suicide could have been avoided if only someone had listened and advised. "I never give anyone advice", quipped a person to me one day. Pity, because that person's advice and counsel could have often saved a plan going awry, a life going wrong. What a ministry we could have if only we counselled a little more!

I know that you might answer that you could give the wrong advice and what then? That is true and the results could be disastrous. Yet, if your advice is based on the Bible, what better advice could you give? Look at the book of Proverbs; there are few areas of life that it does not touch. There is enough counsel in it for you to pass on to change a thousand lives, if heeded. So, pass on the advice given and many will bless God you ever crossed their path.

September 17th

"He who guards his mouth preserves his life and he who opens his lips shall have destruction." Proverbs 13:3

We have all let the sentry sleep at the door of our mouths.

While he sleeps words of jealousy, bitterness, unfair criticism, egotism and cruelty slip past him to do deadly work. They will never return and even should the guard waken up to the seriousness of what has happened all the sentries of all the armies of the world combined couldn't recall the words that got away.

There is a Danish saying which states "A silent man's words are not brought into court". In Spain they have another saying which states "Let not the tongue say what the head shall pay for". In Italy they say "The sheep that bleats is strangled by the wolf". The best sentry at the door of our mouths is the one the Lord sets there. "Set a watch, O Lord, before my mouth; keep the door of my lips". Just remember, silence is never written down.

September 18th

"The simple believes every word but the prudent man considers well his steps." Proverbs 14:15

Gullibility is frightening. Of all the forces that come in inter-personal relationships, Hearsay is one of the most subtlety destructive. Verification is a good antedote to Hearsay. It's a bit like a schoolmaster I had who used to say "all the lies you hear aren't true!".

Gullible people are at the mercy of any adviser and are constantly taken in by the advice of those who are not anchored to the Bible. Prudent people check things out and their unchangeable rule-of-thumb is "assume nothing."

September 19th

"A desire accomplished is sweet to the soul but it is an abomination to fools to depart from evil." Proverbs 13:19

To set your heart on something and then to possess it is sweet. To set your heart on something to possess it, at all costs, is disastrous. It then becomes your master and blinds you to its relative worth. Only Christ is worth having at all costs. Paul counted all things but rubbish that he might win him. Now, there is sweetness.

Fools, of course, refuse to accept the fact that wrongdoing should be shunned. They go for what they want, regardless of what it might cost and if you link up with them you will end up in moral and spiritual ruin. What price, sweetness?

September 20th

"Wisdom is in the sight of him who has understanding but the eyes of a fool are on the ends of the earth." Proverbs 17:24

The other day I stood on a steep hill and looked over a huge valley. I could hardly believe I was there. From that beautiful valley below me, many years ago, a quiet gentleman lifted his pen and wrote some of the most beautiful christian essays ever written. They were written carefully and lovingly and inspired tens of thousands of lives, mine included.

The town was Mosgeil, near Dunedin in New Zealand and as I crossed the Silverstream river and drove into the town I was filled with a sense of deep gratitude for the lovely life once lived there for God.

Frank Boreham's pen became both a searchlight and a flashlamp to me. I leave you with one of his most memorable statements. It sums up today's proverb perfectly. He once said "If you don't find pixies on your own doorstep you'll never find Fairyland". Think about it!

"The poor man uses entreaties but the rich answers roughly."
Proverbs 18:23

This proverb is all about the hardening affect of wealth. Rich men often care little for the poor men at their gates but, as Brer Rabbit used to say, they soon experience the phenomena known as "humble come tumble". The Pharisee might have treated the Publican in our Lord's parable roughly but God despised the Pharisee and justified the Publican.

Watch what wealth, not balanced by God's word in a person's life, can do to that person.

A friend of mine, an undertaker, tells me that when he goes to remove a dead body from some wealthy homes the occupants don't even switch the television off. In poorer districts, he tells me, even the neighbours draw curtains to respect the dead. Selah.

September 22nd

"He who keeps the commandment keeps his soul, but he who is careless of his ways will die." *Proverbs 19:16*

Imagine a game of football with no rules, no sidelines, no scores, no officials, no end and no result. It would be unmitigated nothingness. Millions of people participate in sport and they scream for justice from a referee, a marshall, a steward or a judge at sporting events when people cheat.

Strange, isn't it, how those same people kick against the laws of God? They call God's laws stuffy, too restrictive, mere killjoys. They live their lives apart from them and perish.

The alternative is to trust Christ as Saviour and he will give you power to keep his laws. You will find in the keeping of them there is great reward.

September 23rd

"Wisdom rests quietly in the heart of him who has understanding but what is in the heart of fools is made known." Proverbs 14:33

There are two possible meanings to today's proverb. First, a wise man does not parade his knowledge but a fool's heart is always dancing on his lips. Second, even fools can sometimes recognise that wisdom is to their advantage.

Both meanings are true but I like the little statement which, for me, explains the proverb. It says "the heart of fools is in their mouth; but the mouth of the wise is in their heart". Good, isn't it?

Isn't it wonderful to know that one of God's great communicable attributes is his wisdom? To have it you must first reverence God and second receive God's word. If you do, wisdom will rest in your heart. You and I would be fools to miss it, wouldn't we?

September 24th

"The thoughts of the wicked are an abomination to the Lord but the words of the pure are pleasant." Proverbs 15:26

God's law touches the movement of the mind. Thoughts are heard in heaven. Even before such thoughts become words God knows what motivates them. Evil devices (the thoughts of the wicked) are an abomination to him whereas the words of the pure are pleasing to him.

What kind of words should the words of the pure be? Let's remember that sentry at the door of our lips, again. Imagine the following conversation with him. The sentry asks the vital question "Who goes there?" You answer "Words". "Do they please the Lord?", asks the sentry. If they do the sentry will gladly let them pass. If they don't, don't force the sentry and let them out.

September 25th

"The perverse person is an abomination to the Lord but his secret counsel is with the upright." Proverbs 3:32

Which would you rather have; God's detestation or God's intimate friendship? God hates deviousness but the upright are in his confidence.

I know no better illustration of today's proverb than the story of the Israelite High Priest, Eli. Eli refused to restrain his sons from their devious ways. God, of course, detested the deviousness of Eli's sons and because of Eli's compromise withdrew his intimate friendship from him. The fascinating thing is that that intimate friendship was given to a little boy called Samuel. The child, because of his uprightness was given secret counsel by God. A child in your town or city or townland may be walking closer with God than you or me. Sobering thought?

September 26th

"He who trusts in riches will fall but the righteous will flourish like foliage." Proverbs 11:28

I couldn't believe what I was hearing. He was an older man, making a speech in public and he said "For us to go for £100 to the bank was once a big thing now to go for £100,000 would be no problem". He was boasting and sadly I lived to see the day when to go to the bank for him for £100 was once again a big thing. Don't trust in riches because if you do, as sure as our proverb is true, you will fall. I like what Dr. Graham Scroggie says about the righteous, as found in the first Psalm. Vitality: "a living tree". Security: "planted". Capacity: "by rivers of water". Fertility: "brings forth its fruit". Propriety: "in its season". Perpetuity: "its leaf also shall not wither". Prosperity: "whatsoever he doeth shall prosper".

September 27th

"A man is not established by wickedness but the root of the righteous cannot be moved." Proverbs 12:3

In the Scriptures the ungodly and the wicked are often likened to straw, the righteous to a tree with deep, firm roots. The contrast is between stablity and instability, between freshness and dryness, between roots and rootlessness. They are two totally different qualities of life.

Trees and straw are both vegetable. That is about all they have in common. Trees are alive. Straw is dead. Trees have roots which are constantly nourished by the stream. Straw is uprooted corn. Straw has no source of nourishment and has no means of stability. It is entirely at the mercy of the wind. The water nourishes, the wind blows away. The wind shows the difference. When the storm breaks peoples identity is revealed. How will it find you?

September 28th

"A true witness delivers souls but a deceitful witness speaks lies."
Proverbs 14:25

There is a time to keep quiet and a time to speak up. Some things are better left untold but there are times when a reputation or even a life may be at stake and a word of true witness to the truth can deliver them.

In Jewish law a person was required to witness under oath. That is why when Christ was put under oath by the High Priest to declare who he was he told the truth. Up until then he had been silent. Why did he speak up, even under oath, if he knew that by doing so he was going to die? Because Christ was prepared to die for the truth. So should his followers.

September 29th

"The heart of the righteous studies how to answer but the mouth of the wicked pours forth evil." Proverbs 15:28

Don't you like the little phrase in our proverb which says "studies how to answer"? I heard of a man who was a very keen christian and his friends at work were opposed to christian things. A little baby was born into the christian's home and, unfortunately, the little baby was badly deformed.

At work the christian's workmates gave him a hard time over his child. "Our children are healthy and we blaspheme God", they said. The christian "studied how to answer" for a second or two and then replied, "Well, isn't it a good thing, then, that God allowed the deformed child to be born to me?".

"Do not let your heart envy sinners but in the fear of the Lord continue all day long; for surely there is a hereafter and your hope will not be cut off." Proverbs 22:17-18

Do you want to learn how to deepen your life, not just to lengthen it? Birthdays, you know, tell how long you have been on the road not how far you have travelled. Don't be brainwashed by Satan into wasting your time envying those who have "missed the mark" (the Bibles definition of sinners) but "find the mark" by trusting Christ as Saviour and Lord and continuing in awe and intimate knowledge of him all day long.

Such a lifestyle will not be a disappointment for, as Chrysostom has put it, "If one man should suffer all the sorrows of all the saints in the world, yet they are not worth one hour's glory in heaven". The future belongs to those who belong to God. This is hope and it will not be cut off.

OCTOBER

Righteousness exalts a nation. True? Of course it does, but it isn't news. The media, of course, finds righteousness and the righteous rather dull and wickedness much more fascinating. Ten thousand families may lead a quiet afternoon in your town but if one of them gets in a fight and burns their house down, the nation will know about it before the night is through. This month, though, we want to concentrate on proverbs about righteousness and we shall find it is much more far reaching than first imagined. Right action and fair dealing between people and conformity to God's will is what righteousness is about in Proverbs. Let's explore. If obeyed in your family and in mine such righteousness could, under God, be contagious. It might even become a glorious national epidemic!

October 1st

"The path of the just is like the shining sun that shines even brighter onto the perfect day. The way of the wicked is like darkness; who do not know what makes them stumble."
Proverbs 4:18

This is Keatsian weather, isn't it? Autumn was for John Keats the season which was the "close bosomed friend of the maturing sun". Light is an image of moral goodness and speaks of beauty, joy, expansion and a very bright future. As the sun's light matures from dawn to its noon time brightness so is the path of the just person. That person comes right out of doubt into clear conviction and is conformed to Christ's image.

The secret of such a quality of life is keeping one's eye upon the Saviour and trusting in His righteousness to save and not our own. Then comes a deep, deep desire to be like Him. That is God's way of making the christian holy. We shall, of course, be satisfied when we awake with His likeness. A perfect day, indeed.

October 2nd

"Blessings are on the head of the righteous but violence covers the mouth of the wicked." Proverbs 10:6-7

Christians are not stoics, are they? Stoicism is a heathen philosophy which taught that you do not show emotion in the face of tragedy. Stoics believe that the stiff upper lip is the thing to cover emotion. Christians believe the opposite. They try to follow what their Saviour taught them, namely, to weep with those that weep. They do not believe that they should go around with a permanent grin on their faces.

A sinful life, though, does affect how a person looks. This proverb is saying that the man's evil is written all over his face. So, of course, are the blessings of God on believer's lives. They cannot hide them. It is interesting that the word blessing in Hebrew is never found in the singular. Why? Because they believed there is no such thing as a singular blessing; when one comes it brings others with it. Hallelujah!

October 3rd

"The name of the Lord is a strong tower; the righteous run to it and are safe." Proverbs 18:10

Colin Weldon, of Chariots of Fire fame said, after the film's success, "I have bought a bit of peace in the country". He meant he had bought a new house hoping to get far from the madding crowds ignoble strife. Who could blame him?

Yet, as Kidner said, "It is not the man of God but the man of property who must draw on his imagination". No matter how lovely your home you know that nothing in this world is ultimately secure. The name of the Lord is the only strong tower. It signifies all that God is in himself, his attributes, his love, his mercy, his kindness. He is a sure refuge in the storms of life. In him the righteous are not removed from trouble but are set above it.

Run to that refuge, christian, today.

October 4th

"He stores up sound wisdom for the upright; he is a shield to those who walk uprightly; he guards the paths of justice, and preserves the way of the saints." Proverbs 2:7-8

How many people in this world have plenty of money, have plenty of opportunities to make more, are healthy, live in comfortable surroundings and yet their lives are an absolute mess? They have brains and education but they just do not know how to handle life. Our proverb tells us that those who know the Lord know how to live. The Lord gives them sound sense (wisdom) in how to handle all that life brings.

The wisdom given leads to an upright walk, and, goes along a path of justice. Notice the words "guards" and "preserves". Lean hard on them, today.

If the Lord is your "guard" and your "preserver" what are you afraid of?

"To punish the righteous is not good, nor to strike princes for their uprightness." Proverbs 17:26

Religious persecution has always been a feature of human history. Take the 12 apostles. According to Fox's Book of Martyrs, Matthew was slain in Ethiopia in AD60, Matthias was beheaded, Andrew was crucified to a transversed cross, Mark was dragged to pieces by the people of Alexandria, Peter, Bartholomew, and Simeon were all crucified, Thomas was thrust through with a spear, Luke was hanged on an olive tree and John was the only one to die a natural death.

What could we say of Tyndale, Ridley, Latimer, Cranmer, Judson of Burma, the christians of Uganda in recent years or the christians at Darkley in Co. Armagh? The list is endless. Are you being persecuted for your faith? "Rejoice and be exceeding glad", said Christ, "for great is your reward in Heaven". Great means great. It's a promise.

"The hope of the righteous will be gladness but the expectation of the wicked will perish." Proverbs 10:28

Why are the righteous and the wicked contrasted so starkly and as being so irreconcilable in our proverb? The answer lies in the difference between what is temporal and what is eternal. The wicked base everything on what is temporal. They know that they are finished if that goes. To quote F. Scott Fitzgerald the famous American novelist who said when dying of alcoholism "What if this night prefigured the night after death ... no choice, no road, no hope - only the endless repetition of the sordid and semi-tragic?"

What a difference when the Apostle Paul said "The time of my departure is at hand. I have fought the good fight, I have finished the race, I have kept the faith. Finally, there is laid up for me the crown of righteousness, which the Lord, the righeous judge, will give to me on that day and not to me only but also to all who have loved his appearing". Don't be a fool and stake everything you've got on the temporal.

October 7th

"A righteous man regards the life of his animal, but the tender mercies of the wicked are cruel." Proverbs 12:10

Duncan Donaldson was, without question, Airdrie's wild man. Drunken so often he was, unfortunately, famed for his drinking bouts. He used to take the sweet counter at Woolworths with one shove and several policemen could not hold him.

One evening Duncan accepted Christ as personal Saviour and walked quietly home. For a long time the wild man from Airdrie had more or less kicked open the front door of his home at night in a drunken stupor. Tonight was different, though. He quietly opened his front door, and, do you know what? His own dog bit him!

October 8th

"A righteous man who falters before the wicked is like a murky spring and a polluted well." Proverbs 25:26

Today I travelled from the little town of Marton to the city of New Plymouth in New Zealand. It was about a three hour journey in the bus and rounding a bend I noticed on a hillside a herd of goats and a flock of sheep, mixed. It lead me to think

217

of God's word through Ezekiel, "Behold I shall judge between sheep and sheep, between rams and goats. Is it too little for you to have drunk of the clear waters that you must foul the residue with your feet? As for my flock they eat what you have trampled with your feet and drink what you have fouled with your feet".

Today's proverb warns us that if a righteous person compromises with the wicked it will affect those who have learned to rely on him. The polluted stream still flows on, you know.

Think about it.

"The wicked earns deceptive wages but he who sows righteousness gets a true reward." Proverbs 11:18

The Proverbs is not a book of manners. It deals with manners and personal relationships and attitudes but, above all, this book offers a key to life. Everything is judged by the question "Is this wise or is it foolish?" Our proverb is pointing us to someone who is perhaps a cheat, a liar, a swindler, a bribe taker; his work is riddled with laziness and inconsistency. Is he wise?

Certainly not. Human conduct is viewed as a sowing, followed by a reaping. The gain of the wicked is deceptive, it is illusory. It is temporary and ultimately full of dissatisfaction. The person who sows righteous acts has, ultimately, a sure reward. To change the metaphor "What we weave in time we will wear in eternity".

"The evil will bow before the good and the wicked at the gates of the righteous." Proverbs 14:19

Joseph. Who would ever have thought that his brothers would have needed him before he needed them? No one. They tried to kill him, but, they were to come to a day when they had to bow at his gates and plead for their very lives. The same will be true of our Lord Jesus who will one day be vindicated and when every knee shall bow and every tongue confess that Jesus Christ is Lord.

The same is also true of goodness, ultimately. It will be vindicated. God will bring your right action and wise judgements to shine as the noonday sun. You wait and see. The final victory of good over evil is assured. However successful evil people may appear to be they will finally succumb to the righteous. It's a promise.

"To do righteousness and justice is more acceptable to the Lord than sacrifice." Proverbs 21:3

Note that it was Solomon who wrote this proverb. His greatest work was to build a temple in which sacrifice was to be offered to the Lord. You could have excused him if he had preferred the ceremonial to the moral. But Solomon was not "famous concerning the name of the Lord" for nothing. He knew the Lord and knew that he preferred righteousness to sacrifices, any day, any century.

The Lord preferred the penitent tax gatherer and harlot to the much sacrificing but legal, hard hearted Pharisee. Christ did away with sacrifices by the sacrifice of himself. Clean hands and a pure heart are what God prefers.

October 12th

"The wicked flee when no one pursues but the righteous are bold as a lion." Proverbs 28:1

Today's proverb is about the unreasoning terror of an uneasy conscience. Chrysostom succinctly comments "Such is the nature of sin that it betrays while no one finds fault; it condemns whilst no one accuses, it makes the sinner a timid being, one that trembles at a sound and just as it would be impossible to flee from himself, so neither can he escape the persecuter within but wherever he goeth he is scourged".

The person whose conscience is at rest is entirely different. That person knows God is with them. The lion is not afraid when other animals rise against him because he knows he is stronger. Greater is he who is in you, i.e. Christ, than he who is in the world, i.e. Satan. Christ forgives, cleanses you and makes you strong. Let the lion loose. Onward!

October 13th

"An unjust man is an abomination to the righteous and he who is upright in the way is an abomination to the wicked." Proverbs 29:27

Your choice of friends reveals your choice of path. That is the clear teaching of this proverb. As starlings fly with starlings, ravens with ravens, swallows with swallows, so people fall into types and those types tend to flock together.

If your choice of friends reveals your choice of path, how much more your choice of partner? "Do not be unequally yoked together with unbelievers", warns the Scriptures. The very man who wrote this proverb showed how he veered off the path of God's will for his life by the partners he chose and he, the wisest man in all the earth, became an effeminate fool. "His wives", comments the Bible, "turned his heart after other gods and his heart was not loyal to the Lord his God". Is yours?

October 14th

"He who follows righteousness and mercy finds life, righteousness and honour." Proverbs 21:21

The word "mercy" in our proverb can be translated "devoted love", "fidelity" and "loyalty". As we saw in yesterday's proverb, where your loyalty lies is very important. If you find acceptance with God, as you most certainly can in Christ, you can then stand before him as his loyal, faithful subject.

Look at the promises associated with such loyalty in our proverb; you will find life as it really should be, you will find righteousness as a gift of God, and honour, for "whom he justified them he also glorified" (Romans 8:30). I'd follow righteousness and mercy if I were you.

October 15th

"The silver-haired head is a crown of glory, if it is found in the way of righteousness." Proverbs 16:31

There are a lot of crowns which people seek in this life; crowns of fame, rank, wealth and beauty. It has been well observed that what is spent in winning them is often far more valuable than the good for which the sacrifice is made and they give less satisfaction than the pursuer ever imagined.

I talked to a very wealthy old man one day who was very near to death and I tried to comfort him with the Scriptures. He mocked me. There was no glory in that grey head I can tell you. But the righteous old? They reflect an honourable past, an excellent present, and a glorious future.

Such an old age is not to be despised; it is an inspiration. It holds a torch to the rising generation. When it comes, may we hold it high.

October 16th

"The wicked is banished in his death but the righteous has a refuge in his death." Proverbs 14:32

It is worth emphasising that the biggest battles come when you are old. Youth has its problems but when you are old and your friends are passing away around you Satan taunts you in a new way. He no longer tempts you with the pleasures of sin because you have been along those cul-de-sacs. What he does now is to whisper "And-where-is-your-God-now"?

The answer is that he is right there beside you. The last plague that Pharoah endured was darkness. Belshazzar's knees knocked together as he faced death. For the godless there is nowhere to hide in death. For those trusting in Christ, if they live today it is another day to serve the Lord, but, if they die, it is an eternal day to serve him; it is a praise-the-Lord-anyway situation!

October 17th

"The righteousness of the blameless will direct his way around, but the wicked will fall by his own wickedness". Proverbs 11:5

It is a seriously deadly thing to be blinded by passion and pleasure. They will, if not watched, take your money from you, make you neglect your business and sap strength of your mind and body. Make no mistake that people who are given to pure pleasure seeking in life are cruel and heartless. It ruined the Roman empire because their pleasure became a fiend. It has ruined more than the Romans.

The righteous, not blinded by passion or pleasure follow a safe and direct path. The wicked, losing the sight of their conscience, stumble and fall. Watch indulgence like a hawk.

October 18th

"He who trusts in his riches will fall but the righteous will flourish like foliage." Proverbs 11:28

There was once a young Arab who served a young American at a table in Beirut. According to my friend George Hoffman the Arab was, to his knowledge, not able to read or write. He spoke to the American and asked him if he would like to see around the city. He readily agreed.

In the middle of the tour the young Arab spoke to the American about the Lord Jesus and the Gospel. "I know all about that", the American replied quietly. There in a city, blasted apart with trouble, the Arab lead the American to Christ. The young Arab was certainly, according to today's proverb, like foliage. But who was the young American? Dr. Billy Graham's son.

October 19th

'The wicked shall be a ransom for the righteous and the unfaithful for the upright.' Proverbs 21:18

Don't get a swelled head if the Lord uses you because he uses some mighty strange people. He used the heathen Cyrus to free the exiled Jews in Babylon. His invading armies surrounded and got into the seemingly impregnable city and the repatriated Jews were as those who dreamed. King Artaxerxes was certainly not a believer but look how God used him to help Nehemiah do the work God called him to do. A radio station in Monte Carlo built to send out Nazi propaganda now houses the famed christian radio station Trans World Radio. "Since you were precious in my sight you have been honoured ... I will give men for you and people for your life" (Isaiah 43:4). Amazing verse, isn't it? It is a comfort that it is also a promise which God keeps.

October 20th

"Whoever causes the upright to go astray in an evil way, he himself will fall into his own pit." Proverbs 28:10

Let this promise of God warn any reader against leading anyone astray. Even if it be a child that is corrupted, the Saviour taught that it was better for the corrupter that a millstone were hung around his neck and he were drowned in the depths of the sea. Let all teachers remember that Christ said "Whoever therefore breaks one of the least of these commandments, and teaches men so, shall be called least in the kingdom of heaven; but whoever does and teaches them, he shall be called great in the kingdom of heaven". (Matthew

5:19). Where in Scripture is there a more powerful warning than the words of the Saviour when he said "Woe to you Scribes and Pharisees, hypocrites! For you travel land and sea to win one proselyte, and when he is won, you make him twice as much a son of hell as yourselves"? May God preserve all of us from leading anyone, anywhere astray.

October 21st

"The righteous man walks in his integrity; his children are blessed after him." Proverbs 20:7

What kind of legacy would you like to leave your children? The memory of the smell of cigarette smoke instead of lavender, of suddenly bursting in on you to find you on your knees in prayer, or, you pushing them away because you must go to yet another cocktail party?

You could leave your children a mansion and £1 million each in the bank and their memory of you be frightening. I tell you, father, if you don't go hunting with your son, today, as you promised, as sure as today's proverb, you will go hunting for him on another day.

October 22nd

"When the righteous rejoice, there is great glory; but when the wicked arise, men hide themselves." Proverbs 28:12

When Iraq's President Saddam Hussein recently attacked Kuwait and gobbled it up, the world held its breath. His hero, is apparently Nebuchadnezzar and he recently had himself photographed in a replica of Nebuchadnezzar's war chariot. Hussein is also rebuilding the city of Babylon. The solemn

225

lesson of Nebuchadnezzar's live was the fact that his pride led him to live like an animal. Animals don't use serviettes or napkins and never say please or thank you. If they want it, they grab it. The law of the jungle is that the strongest wins. People hide from such people.

"Human life means nothing to him", said a senior British Diplomat of Hussein. Exactly. Yet in Nebuchadnezzar's day when Daniel went into the den of lions the law of the jungle did not rule. God reversed it. When the men who did believe in it were thrown in they were eaten before their bodies hit the ground. The Bible is very explicit on the matter. We rejoice in this uncertain world that the coming Messiah that Daniel pointed to will once again reverse the law of the jungle and the lion shall lie down with the lamb. What a day. Praise God!

October 23rd

"In the way of righteousness is life and in its path there is no death." Proverbs 12:28

Life and death in the Book of Proverbs are not just saying that good conduct lengthens life and bad conduct shortens it; they are also to be understood qualitatively.

Righteousness or the lack of it effects us socially, personally, psychologically, morally, and spiritually. Put in simple terms if you live for the Lord your pathway in life will be marked by your living life to the full, as God sees life being lived to the full. You will enjoy this fulness despite all your circumstances. You will be "alive" in a way the unbeliever won't; they will be missing true life and living. That both pathways lead out into two very different existences in eternity is clearly taught in Scripture. Your labour, christian, is not in vain in the Lord.

"All the words of my mouth are with righteousness; nothing crooked or perverse is in them." Proverbs 8:8

Wisdom is speaking. The person who knows wisdom shows it on his or her tongue. In the utterances of wisdom there is nothing crooked, no distortion of the truth, all is straightforward and direct.

You will find that a lot of crooked and perverse things in our tongues stem from grumbling and murmuring. Murmuring leads to discontent which leads to covetness which leads to downright iniquity. The answer is to know the Lord and to be content and thankful.

I read about a man who asked the Estate Agent to read him the advertisement he had commissioned him to place in order to sell his estate. When he heard it he said "I don't think I'll sell after all. I have been looking for an estate like that all my life and I didn't know that I owned it!" Selah.

"The righteous sings and rejoices." Proverbs 29:6

Amazing, isn't it, how little lines of what you read stick in your mind? I remember reading once what G. Campbell Morgan said about the church at Ephosus which had left her "first love" for the Lord. Pointing out that the church was faultily faultless, icily regular and splendidly null the great Bible teacher summed up the Lord's letter to the church with the little statement "There was no song at the unusual hour".

Do you raise a song to the Lord at an unusual hour? In the car? The shower? As you walk by the beach? As you lie in your bed in the middle of the night? I trust your praise is not limited to local church services. Let's get back to first-love singing at unusual hours. Those who wish to sing can always find a song.

October 26th

"A wicked man hardens his face but as for the upright, he establishes his way." Proverbs 21:29

I stood in Bluff recently. It is the southernmost town in the southern hemisphere. Next stop is McMurdo Sound in the Antarctic and my, was it cold! This proverb, though, is about another kind of bluff. There are lots of people can put-a-face-on-it and bluff their way in life. Before long, though, they are caught. If you don't live according to sound principles a bold face won't take you through.

The wicked may harden their face and be shameless to rebuke or soft feeling. They refuse counsel. The righteous, though, act only after careful thought. They study the circumstances and are opposed to the rash, unyielding stubbornness of the wicked. So, christian, proceed today with caution. I am going out tonight, God willing, to preach for the 68th time on this tour of New Zealand. Tomorrow night, is my final and 70th message of the tour and I am very well aware that in these final hours if I preach in my own strength at the last few services I could blow the rest. This proverb applies to me too, you know. Let's not be stubborn to Gods leading and go our own way. Selah.

October 27th

"Righteousness exalts a nation but sin is a reproach to any people." Proverbs 14:34

It is a rather frightening thought that at the moment in Britain the two top swear words are "God" and "Christ". Is it any wonder our nation is in the state that it is in? When God's name is not respected look what happens in the areas of integrity, authority, abortion, education and government. The proverb, though, gives us the answer. It tells us that righteousness exalts a nation and any nation is only as good as its individuals.

I often think of Suzanna Wesley who had 19 children. She had to put an apron over her head in order to pray. Her children knew not to disturb her when so covered! From behind that apron came a thousand hymns for the church and nation through her influence on her son Charles. Her son John saved England, under God, from the French Revolution by his Gospel preaching. A nations turnaround begins with the family. It begins at your heart and mine. May righteousness in our homes lead our nation to an exaltation worth having.

October 28th

"Riches do not profit in the day of wrath but righteousness delivers from death." Proverbs 11:4-5

I often think of Howard Hughes the incredibly rich American who lived his last years with uncut finger nails in a room cut off from reality watching his favourite film, "Ice Station Zebra" hundreds and hundreds of times. The Methodist minister who buried him chose as his text "We brought nothing into this world and it is certain we will take nothing out". Brave man.

To miss true life is the real menace of death. As Kidner says "A man can stray into its territory and find himself among its citizens before he ever quits this earth"; the sinner, in the house of folly, "Knoweth not that the dead are there; that her guests are in the depths of Sheol" (Proverbs 9:18).

It is a fact that burdens are lifted at Calvary. There, true righteousness is found by hiding in the Saviour's side. If you trust Him as Saviour He cancels the wages of sin long before the grave. Do you have this righteousness? If not, why not?

October 29th

"The tongue of the righeous is choice silver; the heart of the wicked is worth little." Proverbs 10:20

Again and again the importance of the connection between heart and tongue is established in the Book of Proverbs. What you say directly reflects what you are. Your words are worth just what you are worth. If your life contradicts your words no one will lay any store by what you say, no matter how eloquently you may put it.

How many people do you know who say memorable things, helpful things, choice things? So much of what is said in life is a barren superfluity of words. Meditate often in your heart upon Christ, christian, and see what happens to your words. Go on, try it.

October 30th

"The highway of the upright is to depart from evil; he who keeps his way preserves his soul." Proverbs 16:17

An old story tells of a peddler who when he came to a crossroads, would throw a pointed stick into the air and then take the road indicated by the point where the stick had fallen to earth. When the peddler took a fancy to a certain direction, however, he would throw the stick into the air repeatedly until its point indicated the road he wanted to take.

Much better the advice of Robert Frost who said "I came to a crossroads in the woods and I took the road less travelled by". The choice of deciding to always depart from evil will guide you as no other choice. It is certainly, in this evil world, a road less travelled by. Which choice have you made, today?

October 31st

"The root of the righteous yields fruit." Proverbs 12:12

Recently in one of the fruit bowls of New Zealand, the Hastings-Napier area, an orchard owner took me out among his trees. He had a very "high-tec" pruning operation with a movable platform almost akin to a high-rise moon buggy. He got me to try to operate it and I think I nearly pruned myself! It was fun! The fruit that he grew, though, was delicious.

As the Lord prunes your life and mine may our root in the Spirit yield those peaceable fruits of righteousness; love, joy, peace, long suffering, gentleness, goodness, faith, meekness and temperance. There is no law anywhere in the world against them. Let your life, this month and every month be a harvest of righteous fruit. May they say of you that "Your root is showing".

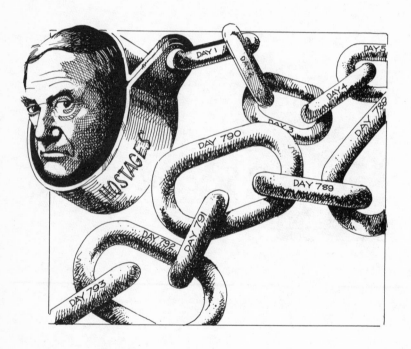

Sadaam Hussein, at the time of writing, who has just "gobbled up" the state of Kuwait with his Iraqui forces says that he is using the thousands of foreigners trapped in Kuwait as a "human shield", against the international naval blockade that surrounds his coastline. The United States President, of course, and other western leaders do not see their trapped citizens as a "human shield" but as hostages which are being used as pawns in Hussein's ambitions. This month, as I write, protection, help and succour of nationals is a very big issue. As long as human life lasts it always will be.

The protection, help and succour of the people of God is also a big issue in the Book of Proverbs. Let's look at the principles involved. As winter comes upon us, let's see what protection and help is available for those whose citizenship is in Heaven.

November 1st

"He stores up sound wisdom for the upright; he is a shield to those who walk uprightly; he guards the paths of justice, and preserves the way of his saints." Proverbs 2:7-8

There can be no doubt that a christian, in this world, is very vulnerable. To live for Christ in a world that is full of selfishness and envy leaves a person who follows the way of Christ wide open for abuse, ridicule and attack.

Those who have seen christians and the christian church as weak and easy to exploit had better take note of history. The Romans saw the christian church as insignificant but where is the Roman Empire now? It is mere Mediterranean rubble. A look across the 20th century has shown the same pattern, from Idi Amin's Uganda to Gobachov's Russia. Hours of Soviet television is now devoted to spiritual matters and church activities. The church is now such a force that the Soviet government cannot afford to push it into opposition. Solzhenitzn, who became a christian in the Gulag of Stalin has had his Russian citizenship restored. It is true that christians may be vulneable but their shield is the Lord. What better ultimate protection? Even the very gates of Hell will not prevail against his church.

November 2nd

"Do not be afraid of sudden terror, nor of trouble from the wicked when it comes; for the Lord will be your confidence, and will keep your foot from being caught." Proverbs 3:25-26

Fear often grips me. Fear of people, fear of Satan, fear of circumstances beyond my control, fear that after having taught others I myself, by foolish action, could become useless in God's service. Many people have fear of losing their jobs, of accidents, of illness, of financial disaster. Even before your feet hit the floor in the mornings you could be filled with fear.

The christians confidence is the Lord. He counteracts fear. Listen to His promise; "There will be", he said, "signs in the sun, in the moon, and in the stars; and on the earth distress of nations, with perplexity, the sea and the waves roaring, men's hearts failing them from fear and the expectation of those things which are coming on the earth. Now when you see these things begin to happen, look up and lift up your heads because your redemption draws near". So, christian, look up and lift up your head today. As Henry Law said "If you stood alone, it would be presumption to hope. Because you are not alone, it is an offence to tremble."

"The fear of the wicked will come upon him, and the desire of the righteous will be granted, when the whirlwind passes by the wicked is no more, but the righteous has an everlasting foundation." Proverbs 10:24-25

If the Lord gave you every request you made of Him it certainly would not be good for you, would it? Even our best desires can be mixed up with wrong motivation. Even "in the multitude of words, sin is not lacking", wrote Solomon. It is very comforting to know that God separates that which is evil from that which is good in our asking. God gives to our need rather than our greed. Desire for more property, you know, is often the rich mans poverty. As the old saying goes, "He who needs £5,000 to live is just as poor as he who needs but £5"! Let our desires be submitted to the sovereign will of God; don't be afraid to talk to him about them. Look up, for God looks down. When your eyes meet His, your whole pattern of desires are transformed. If you doubt it, ask Peter.

"The way of the Lord is strength for the upright." Proverbs 10:29

God's promise is that He gives power to the weak and to those who have no might He increases strength. This doesn't imply that we do not bring the best of our mind and strength to the tasks that face us, though, does it? I know that spiritual blessing is "Not by might nor by power but by my spirit sayeth the Lord" but if I am going to preach, for example, on the Book of Ezekiel it doesn't mean I won't have to study

Ezekiel first. I must prepare as if there were no Holy Spirit and then preach as if I had never prepared.

You may not be a preacher but your work, christian, is just as important as any preachers. You and I must work as if we are going to live for ever and pray as if we were going to die today. So, work as if all depended on you and pray because all depends on God.

November 5th

"In the fear of the Lord there is strong confidence, and his children will have a place of refuge. The fear of the Lord is a fountain of life, to avoid the snares of death." Proverbs 14:26-27

"The fear of the Lord" is the motto of the book of Proverbs. It is the beginning of wisdom, the first and controlling principle of a godly life. It is not a phase one passes through. It is a worshipping submission to God. It is a relationship in the fullest sense, and, in our Proverb, is a fortress and a fountain at the same time. The fear of the Lord protects but is also full of vitality.

The emphasis of the proverb is that a parent who is governed by the fear of the Lord is showing his children a path of life that is, by far, stronger and better. It will protect them when the crisis of life hits them. They will know where to run. Better than the old school tie, better than a huge bank account, better than the glitzy socialite round, is a lifestyle rooted and guided by the fear of the Lord. It even protects from the devils subtle snares.

Is the fear of the Lord your guiding principle? If it isn't you don't realise the mortal danger you are in.

'The eyes of the Lord are in every place, keeping watch on the evil and the good." Proverbs 15:3

Eye-servants are eye sores; aren't they? They are unbearable people because you know that the moment the boss's back is turned they will be wasting his time. In our lives we must never become eye-servants because another eye is watching us which keeps a diligent gaze on the evil as well as the good. His eye is never shut in sleep and sees not only our outward behaviour but right into our hearts. "Hell and Destruction are before the Lord, so how much more the hearts of the sons of men?", writes Solomon.

The proverb, though, is not just a warning, it is a great comfort. Is someone slandering you? Are you being misunderstood? All you did was meant for good but it is being twisted by others to mean the very opposite. Do not fear, the Lord's eyes are in every place. He sees. If you lose a penny for Christ he will give you a pound. Bank on it.

November 7th

"Thorns and snares are in the way of the perverse; he who guards his soul will be far from them." Proverbs 22:5

We bring a lot of trouble in life on our own heads, don't we? The teaching of today's proverb is that a lot of thorns and snares in life are avoidable; you can protect yourself from them. How? Well, touch a galled horse and he will kick you, won't he? There are perverse, twisted people in this world and, if you get too close to them, they will hurt you. Never look for pippins on a crabtree: sour yields sour and it is stupidity to look for sweetness from such a source.

Successive mild winters have seen a massive increase in wasps in our country and each nest contains up on 30,000 worker wasps! You would be a fool to put your hand into such a nest, wouldn't you? Consider your own peace then before you start to meddle with those who are perverse. Keep far from them. By doing so you will guard your very soul.

November 8th

"Every word of God is pure; he is a shield to those who put their trust in Him. Do not add to His words lest he reprove you and you be found a liar." Proverbs 30:5-6

God is where he was. He doesn't change his place and he certainly doesn't change his power. You can trust his every word because it is a tried word. Just as silver is tried in a furnace, so God's word has stood the test of the ages. Not a single syllable of it will fail to accomplish the purpose for which it was sent. Every word of God is pure, so believe him and you will find him a shield. When he opens a door for you he promises no man can shut it. Trust him. You couldn't trust a fox with your young chickens, nor could you trust a smooth sea, never to speak of even trusting yourself. So, cultivate a wise distrust of people and an unbending trust in God and you will win through. At the same time, though, don't forget to lock your stable door.

November 9th

"A man's gift maketh room for him." Proverbs 18:16

Learn it, and learn it well; you don't need to manipulate and push and shove to get your gift recognised. If God gifts you, he will give you a sphere in which to exercise that gift. From the most obscure and narrow circumstances your gift will, in the course of your life, make room for you.

Check out these people in the Bible as a special study. Read how God crossed their lives with circumstances by which their gifts surfaced. They pulled no strings. Then opportunities came, in God's providence and thousands were blessed. Check them out: Eliezer, Joseph, Deborah, Abigail, Nehemiah, Ruth, Anannias, Aquila and Priscilla. You don't need to live in a big house, go to a top flight university, have loads of money in order to make progress. Your gift will make room for you; naturally, quietly, unobtrusively, certainly. Treasure your gift. Develop your gift. Be patient. God will match it with the appropriate circumstance.

November 10th

"Do not despise the chastening of the Lord nor detest his correction; for whom the Lord loves he corrects, just as a father the son in whom he delights." Proverbs 3:11-12

When, and if, you trusted Christ as Saviour the penal judgment against you, and your sin, was lifted. You will never be in Hell for you have indeed discovered that the greatest barrier to Hell is the cross of Calvary. The punishment for your sin fell on that sacred one and hiding in him you are now free from it. That freedom, though, now brings you under a new principle; the principle is that you are free not to do as you want but as He wants. That is true freedom.

That freedom involves discipline and that discipline involves the chastening of the Lord. He has his own ways and means of correcting us and bringing us into line when we

241

wander. In fact chastening is a sign of the Lord's love, it is a clear proof that we are his. It is very easy to despise and detest it, to try to thwart it and run from it. Don't. Be exercised by it and let it lead you to better days. It always will. It's a promise. As Fred Mitchell said "The Heavenly Father has no spoiled children. He loves them too much to allow that".

November 11th

"The prudent man foresees evil and hides himself but the simple pass on and are punished." Proverbs 22:3

I always remember an interview on the BBC with David McIlveen. Bravely he stood up against a film which was being networked across the nation which contained material highly offensive to christians. The inevitable question came, "Have you seen the film?" No, he hadn't. "Then how can you criticise a film you haven't seen?" "I don't need to", he replied, "The posters show very clearly what material is contained in the film". Mr. McIlveen was applying today's proverb to his life. So must we. If your right hand offend you, cut if off, Christ advised. In other words, we even need cultural amputation in these days when sin is often looked upon as an art form.

November 12th

"He who hates covetousness will prolong his days." Proverbs 28:16

There are some people in this life and they covet everything. They see a person's car and they can't let the person enjoy it, they have to covet it. They see a person's house and they can't even sit in it without wanting it for themselves.

They see a person's farm, or business, or gift, or position in life and they light the touch paper of covetousness and burn it to the point of exploding any possibility of a healthy relationship with others.

Man is infinite in what he covets. Let covetousness loose in your life and there is no knowing where it will end; put out its flame in a sea of prayer and lengthen your life. Enjoy what you have, today, and never let your yearnings get ahead of your earnings.

November 13th

"Whoever is a partner with a thief hates his own life; he swears to tell the truth, but reveals nothing." Proverbs 29:24

If you want to open yourself to endless trouble, get in league with a thief. This proverb is a warning to protect you from heartache. Consenting to sin involves guilt and punishment and if you get into fellowship with sin you will soon be sitting in the seat of the scornful. The very first Psalm warns us not to take active advice from the ungodly. You will never find true happiness there.

The ungodly (defined in the Bible as those who are "loose from God") do have their own motto's and codes and philosophies. They are not brainless, by any means. The thing you want to watch is moulding your life according to their pattern and counsel. If you do, they will steal your joy, disturb your peace and lead you astray. Remember, you can't trust them. With the media bombarding you with information from all sorts of corners and from all sorts of situations learn to balance all you read and see with God's word. Remember; there is no sin so great but that a great saint may fall into it and there is no saint so great but that he could fall into great sin.

"A satisfied soul loathes the honeycomb, but to a hungry soul every bitter thing is sweet." Proverbs 27:7

The attitude you adopt is often dictated by the level of comfort you chose. How often have you seen "fat" christians get even "fatter", never having to be exposed to the storm of persecution or the winds of godless thinking? They begin to "get used" to their benefits and get "overfed" in their "holy huddle".

Recently a headmaster, away for a week at an educational conference came into a service where I happened to be teaching the Bible. In prayer at a later service he publicly thanked God for the word he had heard preached after a week spent in the environment of humanistic thinking. If you would protect your ministry, preacher or christian teacher, don't just listen to the "holy huddle" as they loathe your honeycomb; concentrate on giving a word to the person who is weary. The "holy huddle" may not like it but the weary sure will. Believe me; concentrate on the weary. Give them your honey and they'll come back for more. I've proved it from one end of the world to the other.

November 15th

"To seek ones glory is not glory." Proverbs 25:27

We live in a day of the C.V. Now, I know that to seek a new job, you need a C.V. I know, I know, but, if you had to read the letters that arrive on my desk from christians trying to get exposure for this para-church organization or that or for this speaker or that, you would know how sick I often feel as the object of their promotion is promoted. It's a bit like something I read recently where someone imagined the disciples approaching the Lord as his huge congregations were dispersing and saying "But, Lord, we've got to get their name and addresses for our mailing list!"

Read today's proverb and it will protect you from glory seeking. It will keep you from false manipulation and from pushing and shoving your own thing to the detriment of exalting Him who, alone, is worthy.

November 16th

"A mans pride will bring him low, but the humble in spirit will retain honour." Proverbs 29:23

Here is a great protector, a humble spirit. Pride rejects that the fear of the Lord is the beginning of wisdom and as has been pointed out, the proud man is at odds with himself (8:36), his neighbour (13:10) and the Lord (16:5). I like what George Thomas, the former Speaker of the House of Commons said when asked how he felt about his elevation to the House of Lords. He replied "I shall still be the same size in the bath!" That's the spirit! The right way to grow is to grow less in your own eyes.

November 17th

"Does not wisdom call and understanding lift up her voice?" Proverbs 8:1

Millions of young people have been very moved by the film "Dead Poets Society". So have I. The English teacher Mr. Keating, a man who has a very strong bias towards the

245

romantic poets and played brilliantly by Robert Williams, stirs his class of boys to grasp life, to be different, to live life instead of just watching it. The boys try it, but disaster strikes as one of the lads, Neill Perry, filled with romanticism comes up against a father who has no time for romantic notions.

The film raises a very big question; are romantics foolish and realists wise? Do you have to be one or the other? I think, quite frankly, you can be both, if you temper all you do with the wisdom found in the Bible. Joseph was a dreamer but no greater realist ever lived. In history few have had such staying power as Joseph's godly, yet romantic life. I've found living for the Lord Jesus and spending time in His service to be a life filled with romance of the very best kind. Something lives in every hue that Christless eyes have never seen. Yet, I have also found that knowing Christ helps me face reality like nothing else does. To escape to Him is, in fact, ultimate reality.

November 18th

"He who has pity on the poor lends to the Lord and he will pay back what he has given." Proverbs 19:17

God is no mans debtor, that's for sure. Our proverb is telling us not to despise the poor and to pity their plight. We must always be kind to them. When we are, we might as well be lending to the Lord. No banking system on earth could compare with his returns.

Notice, though, that you could give all your goods to feed the poor, but, if you don't have love motivating your giving it will profit you nothing. Pity is, you see, akin to love. Have a heart full of pity for the plight of those less fortunate than yourself. You will find that the poor person's hand is the treasury of Christ.

"Where there is no relevation, (vision A.V., R.V.) the people cast off restraint." Proverbs 29:18

There are two types of prophet in the Bible. The first is the classical prophet, who, when speaking was actually speaking the actual words of God. The cannon of Scripture being complete, we don't have such prophets any more. There is a New Testament gift of prophecy, though. As I see it, this is the gift of applying God's word to our times. You know how when you hear a speaker in your local church speaking from the Bible and you say, "How did that person know about me? That word was for me". I reckon that's a present day prophet at work. What such a prophet is saying is absolutely Bible based and not speculative. We desperately need such a word in our world. It brings vision and restraint.

November 20th

"If you faint in the day of adversity, your strength is small." Proverbs 24:10

People can be divided into 3 groups, it is said. There are those who make things happen, those who watch things happen and those who wonder what happened. Which are you? I hope you are among those who make things happen. Wouldn't you rather make history than just read it?

Of course, you'll get flack on such a path, and, as the proverb says, "If you faint in the day of adversity your strength is small". Let faith in God be your strength. Faith is demonstrated by christians who refuse to accept failure as final. "When I cannot live by the faith of assurance I live by the faith of adherence", said Matthew Henry. I call that "going on automatic pilot". When I am afraid I adhere to my implicit belief that God will bring me through whatever cloud I'm in, to His glory. I have never found my faith misplaced and I know I never will. Neither will you.

November 21st

"Do not look on the wine when it is red ... at last it bites likes a serpent, and stings like a vipor. Your eyes will see strange things, and your heart will utter perverse things." Proverbs 23:31-33

I met a diplomat in Geneva once. The son of a preacher, and the High Commissioner for his African nation, he told me that he once bought his father a soft drink on a hot day. Not wishing to offend his father he bought himself a soft drink as well. "Why the soft drink?", said his father, "You are of age now, you can buy what you want". He went and bought himself a beer. He had not drunk very much of the beer whenever his father pointed out to him his uncle, a leading medical Professor at the local university, who was drunk in the hotel grounds where they were sitting. "He is not doing his university any good in his present state, is he?" said the preacher to his son. "He is not doing his own reputation or himself any good in his present state, is he?" "My", the diplomat told me, "that beer I drank was bitter!". There are a whole lot of ways to skin a cat, aren't there?

November 22nd

"He who gives to the poor will not lack, but he who hides his eyes will have many curses." Proverbs 28:27

Open you eyes to the needs of others. Be sensitive. Listen

carefully. Be available. Stay flexible. Don't get stuck in a rut where you can't move, if God is directing you to move here or there use initiative. Become an ice-breaker. Be tactful. Don't barge into helping those in need. Do it with care and courtesy. Always be dignified, but always take advantage of your opportunities.

Don't, our proverb warns, shut your eyes to the needs of others or curses will attend your life. Notice that's a promise. Gilt edged security on earth cannot hinder riches slipping away from you. Put money in the bank of heaven and it will never penalise your trust.

November 23rd

"He who is often reproved and hardens his neck will suddenly be destroyed and that without remedy." Proverbs 29:1

There comes a time when God says "enough". Today's proverb is a solemn warning to protect us from the stupidity of the stubbornness of the rebel.

Again and again God's warnings come before the rebel, the Holy Spirit's convictions urge him to repent and submit to God's goodness and grace. God's wounds, you know, cure; sin's kisses kill. "The rod and reproof give wisdom", says Solomon, "But a child left to himself brings shame on his mother". Even in God's condemnations, comfort is to be found. The rebel, though, refuses to listen. If you don't put yourself into God's hand of mercy you cannot be delivered out of his hand of justice.

November 24th

"If you are wise you are wise for yourself, and if you scoff, you alone will bear it." Proverbs 9:12

It was Paul who wrote "Let each one examine his own work and then he will have rejoicing in himself alone and not in another. For each one shall bear his own load". We have already studied the proverb which says "The heart knows its own bitterness and a stranger does not share its joy". What you are, you are, as Kidner says, "Your character is the one thing you cannot borrow, lend, or escape, for it is you". Ultimately you are the one who gains or loses by the path you choose.

Chose carefully and if you are worried what the crowd will think of you, don't be; they, by and large, don't think about you, at all.

November 25th

"Put away from you a deceitful mouth and put perverse lips far from you." Proverbs 4:24

Attitude. More important than your education, than your bank balance, than your job, than fame or pain, successes or failures is your choice of attitude. When your attitude is right things are transformed around you.

Particularly affected is your mouth. If you get into the habit of being cynical, sarcastic, flippant, and telling half-truths which you don't really mean in the first place, before long that becomes your attitude, your trait, in communication. Change it to an attitude of encouragement, reverence, helpfulness, and dedication to telling the truth and see what happens to your spoken words. It will protect them. A person's heart isn't pure whose tongue is not clean.

"When wisdom enters your heart and knowledge is pleasant to your soul discretion will preserve you; understanding will keep you, to deliver you from the way of evil, from the man who speaks perverse things." Proverbs 2:10-12

Wisdom brings great protection in your life. Moral factors always take first place in the wisdom of the book of Proverbs. You have to be good to be wise and you have to be wise to be good; the two are one.

"The Lord gives wisdom, from his mouth come knowledge and understanding", writes Solomon. Trust Christ as Saviour and imbibe the mind of Christ through Bible study and prayer. Let the saving life of Christ live out through you and you will find that the lifestyles, the talk, the ambitions of evil people will become alien to you. They will be distasteful. If they aren't, something is desperately wrong.

"My son, if you receive my words, and treasure my commands within you, so that you incline your ear to wisdom, and apply your heart to understanding; yes, if you cry out for discernment, and lift up your voice for understanding, if you seek her as silver and search for her as for hidden treasures; then you will understand the fear of the Lord and find the knowledge of God." Proverbs 2:1-5

Notice the verbs in this wonderful passage on the value of wisdom; "receive", "treasure", "incline", "apply", "cry out", "lift up", "seek", "search", "understand", "find". The longer you live the more you will come to realise the incredible value of God's revealed word, the Bible. It is God's heart and mind revealed, and as you study it, christian, you will find two things will happen. You will be filled with awe for God and you will also come into a position of great intimacy with God. As the passage puts it you will "understand the fear of the Lord" and "find the knowledge of God".

Study the verbs again and make them truly active verbs in your life.

November 28th

"To know wisdom and instruction, to perceive the words of understanding." Proverbs 1:2

The word "perceive" in today's proverb, can be translated "insight". To know the Lord gives tremendous insight into every aspect of your life; in private and in public, with the family and within the community.

When Solomon was given opportunity to ask whatever he wanted from the Lord he asked for "an understanding heart". He said he wanted it in order to be able to perceive what was good and what was evil (see 1 Kings 3:9). It was given to him and he became the wisest man in all the earth.

Christian, I do not know what situation you face today but why not ask the Lord just now for the insight to see into the very heart of the situation that troubles you? God will give you the wisdom to see the hollowness of what is carnal and transitory and the glory of what is spiritual and eternal. On such a basis you will see the issues more clearly. Chose the eternal.

"Receive my instruction and not silver, and knowledge rather than choice gold; for wisdom is better than rubies and all the things one may desire cannot be compared with her." Proverbs 8:10-11

If you had all the silver and all the gold in the world but didn't know how to use it wisely, what good would it do you? I read in my newspaper this very day of businessmen driven by greed for money and power, who didn't care about dishonest dealing or the members of the public they represented. They were sent to jail for their behaviour. One of them had a personal fortune estimated at £500 million. The case brought against them cost an estimated £25 million; the most expensive case in British legal history. How many more people with money and power are wrecked on the shores of life's ocean because they are driven by the carnal and immediate and do not know the glory of what is spiritual and eternal? Should God grant you riches, fame and success, don't run scared or feel guilty. Just stay balanced by keeping eternal values in view. The man who wrote today's proverb eventually set those values aside and wrecked his testimony. It doesn't make the proverb any less valuable, does it?.

November 30th

"Now therefore, listen to me, my children, for blessed are those who keep my ways. Hear instruction and be wise, and do not distain it. Blessed is the man who listens to me, watching daily at my gates, waiting at the posts of my doors. For whoever finds me finds life, and obtains favour from the Lord; but he who sins against me wrongs his own soul; all those who hate me love death."
Proverbs 8:32-36

Let us drive wisdom's appeal home to our hearts as November days finish. "He who has the Son has life; he who does not have the Son does not have life", wrote John. It's as simple as that. There's life and death in it. As E. Stanley Jones said, "The cross is the key. If I lose the key I fumble. The universe will not open to me. But with the key in my hand I know I hold its secret". Calvary covers it all.

DECEMBER

It will, for many, be a busy month. For millions it will be an excuse to indulge in alcohol, in partying, in spending as if there were no January, next year. Many will use the birth of Christ as an excuse to try to find happiness in every place but in Christ.

It reminds me of the Mayor of a town who invited me to preach at a Civic Service, once. He was in the habit of inviting speakers to present Christ's claims and Gospel truths at such services. At Christmas he did the same and was, yes, you've guessed it, actually accused to his face of bringing religion into Christmas!

This month I thought it would be a bonus to slip next door to the book of Ecclesiastes and study some more proverbs Solomon wrote about a journey he once took to try to find the secret of happiness. If you listen to and act on his conclusions it will save you a lot of searching and needless heartbreak. The story is intriguing and it could lead you to the happiest Christmas you have ever known.

December 1st

"The words of the Preacher, the son of David, king in Jerusalem 'Vanity of vanities', says the Preacher; 'Vanity of vanities, all is vanity.'" Ecclesiastes 1:1-2

Life without God is despair personified. Learn it before you have to learn it. There is nowhere you can go, no book you can read, no country you can visit, no drink you can drink, no appetite you can seek to satisfy, no car you can drive, no home you can live in, no place of education you can study in, no person you can talk to who can ultimately satisfy you. Don't let anybody tell you otherwise. Only God can meet that need.

It was Charlie Chaplin who once said, "I'm all dressed up and have nowhere to go". "Dressed to die ... with my red veins full of money", wrote Dylan Thomas. He called himself "the drunkest man in the world" and died, wrecked, at 39. Again and again Solomon will warn you; outside of God there is no meaning, no hope and all is emptiness. Believe him.

December 2nd

"One generation passes away, and another comes ... the wind goes toward the south, and turns toward the north, and comes again on its circuit ... all the rivers run into the sea, yet the sea is not full ... there is nothing new under the sun." Ecclesiastes 1:4-9

Solomon is discussing life in a beneath-the-sun perspective. If you live without God life will, ultimately, be boring and monotonous. Generations will come and go, the wind will come and go, the rivers will flow into the sea and evaporate in the sun's heat and go back into rain and snow and form rivers again. Everything will have no purpose if you view it without God. Sadaam Hessein, we are told, wants to be like Nebuchadnezzar. What's new? "The crimes that we call new; John Bunyan had them typed and filed in 1682", wrote Kipling.

I saw a pair of Barker brogues being advertised in a national newspaper, recently. They were photographed sitting on an RAF spitfire! Even advertising in our day goes back to go forward! There is nothing new under the sun. Only the God who lives beyond the sun can make all things new in your life. When a person becomes a christian "old things are passed away and behold all things are become new". No one breaks monotony like the Lord Jesus can! Do you know him?

December 3rd

"The eye is not satisfied with seeing nor the ear filled with hearing ... that which is done is what will be done." Ecclesiastes 1:8

In October 1971 the late Shah of Persia threw a party. 9 Kings, 5 Queens, 16 Presidents, 2 Sultans and an Emperor joined the "bash". He had 61 air conditioned, Persian carpeted tents erected. 165 chefs, 7,700 lbs of meat, a ton of fresh cream, and 25,000 bottles of wine set aside for the comfort of his guests. By the way, 300 wigs and 240 lbs of hairpins took care of the guests hairstyles.

In March 1984 the Sultan of Brunei had 4,000 guests to a party to end all parties on a 350 acre site. The Sultan appeared in a £140,000 Rolls Royce, his wife had a separate, similar model. King Farouk once ordered a new Bentley but by the time it arrived he was too fat to get in! In 1989 Malcolm Forbes had a party in Morocco ... ah, read today's proverb and learn that none but Christ can satisfy.

December 4th

"And I set my heart to know wisdom and to know madness and folly. I perceived that this also is grasping for the wind." Ecclesiastes 1:17

I shall never forget my studies at University, particularly studies in Moral Philosophy. As I started out I was filled with a sense of "now-here-is-fresh-insight-indeed". Plato. Aristotle. Kant. Keigeggard. John Stuart Mill. Sartre. Talk about disillusionment! The more I studied these men the more confused I often became. In fact it is not uncommon to find that many of these thinkers spend their time thinking about what other thinkers think and deciding that they think others are thinking wrong!

Solomon found that even when he knew madness and folly it was as empty as seeking knowledge without God. His Royal Highness, Prince Charles, has put it very well when he said, in his book "A Vision of Britain" that a lot of our problems come with "the denial of God's place in the scheme of things and the substitution of man's infallibility". As C. S. Lewis said "God never plays philosopher with a washer-woman".

December 5th

"I said in my heart 'Come now, I will test you with mirth; therefore enjoy pleasure'; but surely, this also was vanity. I said of laughter, 'It is madness'; and of mirth, 'What does it accomplish?'"
Ecclesiastes 2:1-2

If ever a statement was designed to save you a lot of time, money and ultimate heartbreak, this is it! Here is Solomon with a limitless supply of money and no one to say to him "Sorry, you can't go to it, you can't taste it, or chase it, or buy it". I wish I could write the statement of Solomon's and put it over every kind of pleasure known to man. All of it is empty if not God orientated.

"Yes", said Marilyn Munroe, "there was something special about me, and I knew what it was. I was the kind of girl they found dead in a hall bedroom with an empty bottle of sleeping pills in her hand". She was, at 36. Richard Todd states that Marilyn was once found weeping at the edge of the set as he acted Peter Marshall's Bible sermons for the film "A Man called Peter". I find that infinitely sad, don't you? If you won't learn from Solomon, learn from Marilyn.

December 6th

"I made my works great, I built myself houses ... and indeed all was vanity." Ecclesiastes 2:4-11

There is something about a house. If you are looking for a new one you will find as you pursue your desire that you will get a feeling about houses. You can detest a house, feel neutral about a house, and suddenly, even, feel tremendously at home in a house and say "This is what I want". But don't put too much expectation into it. Ultimately a house is only an inn by the side of the road.

How many a person thinks "If only I could build that dream house designed by that famous architect I would be happy". The answer is, you wouldn't. It is true that money can buy you a house but it cannot buy you a home. Have you ever read Galsworthy's "The Forsyte Saga"? What about Soames, the "man of property"? A more unhappy, dissatisfied character was never created in English literature. Galsworthy never quotes Ecclesiastes but his book is a classic exposition of what it is saying: happiness is not, repeat not, bricks and mortar. Be warned.

December 7th

"I acquired male and female singers, the delights of the sons of men and musical instruments ... and indeed all was vanity." Ecclesiastes 2:8

Music is an international language; from jungle tribes to the Royal Opera House, from Tudor lyres to synthesisers, it breaks through all barriers. The late Professor Blacking, a famous anthropologist in Belfast, used to claim that it is the elitists in music, with their structuring of music, who kill the music in people for, he claimed, music is in everyone.

Solomon wrote 1,000 songs and had the best singers and musical instruments available but he still claimed that, without God, it is empty. It's like Billie Holiday, called the greatest jazz vocalist who ever lived, said, "I'm always making a comeback but nobody ever tells me where I've been". Unless you have a personal knowledge of God even music can't give you peace.

December 8th

"I made myself gardens and orchards and I planted all kinds of fruit trees in them. I made myself water pools from which to water the growing trees of the grove ... indeed, all was vanity."
Ecclesiastes 2:5-6

The most famous Flower Show in the world is the Chelsea Flower Show in London. Every year I love to watch the television programme on "Chelsea" as the glories of formal gardens or tiny alpine gardens, of running brooks and shooting fountains, are discussed and given awards. The roses, the tulips, the lilies, the dahlias, the chrysanthemums, the hydrangea, the pansies, are discussed. We are told that it was brilliant nurserymen who produced this or that new flower. It's all very wonderful but there is not a word about the one who created it all. In fact if the commentators mentioned the Creator they would probably be severely criticised for bringing religion into it! Solomon had a Chelsea all to himself but he says that without knowing God, even the best garden will leave you empty.

December 9th

"Whatever my eyes desired I did not keep from them. I did not withhold my heart from any pleasure." Ecclesiastes 2:10

It is an amazing statement, isn't it? And yes, you've guessed it, Solomon, as Scripture puts it elsewhere, "loved many women". How many? 1,000 (1 Kings 11:3). What was the result? Let's face it honestly and squarely in this age of ours when sex seeps into almost every area of life; did Solomon feel good at last? No. He was bored. The satisfaction of sexual urges are not even sufficient to keep you sane, never to speak of keeping you happy.

So, does sex come into the realm of the knowledge of God in our lives? It certainly does. "God thought of sex before man did", writes John Blanchard, "And when man leaves God out of his sexual thinking he is in trouble". What would people not give to have the word sex set free from every trace of fear, guilt, shame and impurity? It's possible when you obey God and His word on the matter.

December 10th

"I considered all my activities which my hands had done and the labour which I had exerted, and behold all was vanity in striving after wind and there was no profit under the sun."
Ecclesiastes 2:11

The message of the last ten days in our readings is very clear; life without God is empty. Don't let the so called "good life" fool you. You still don't believe me? Then read this.

263

Whenever Richard Cory went to town,
We people on the pavement looked at him;
He was a gentleman from sole to crown,
Clean favoured, and imperially slim.

And he was always quietly arrayed,
And he was always human when he talked;
But still he fluttered pulses when he said,
"Good morning", and he glittered when he walked.

And he was rich - yes, richer than a king,
And admirably schooled in every grace;
In fine, we thought that he was everything,
To make us wish that we were in his place.

So on we worked, and waited for the light,
And went without the meat, and cursed the bread;
And Richard Cory, one calm summer night,
Went home and put a bullet through his head.

E. A. Robinson (1897)

December 11th

"To everything there is a season ... a time to be born and a time to die." Ecclesiastes 3:1-12

All of us have burdens to bear and, let's face it, life is one of them. You didn't ask to come into this world but you are here and existence carries its burden. Are you near to despair? Are you overwhelmed with problems?

Let me gently remind you that God is the great burden bearer (see Isaiah 46:1-4). Isaiah once mocked the gods of Babylon, Nebo and Bel, for the fact that when calamity came on their worshippers they, the gods, had to be carried away!

He taught that we do not have to carry our God; he carries us. Trust Him who has upheld you since birth and says "Even to grey hairs I carry you. I have made, and I will bear; even I will carry and will deliver you". It's a promise.

December 12th

"A time to plant and a time to pluck what is planted."
Ecclesiastes 3:2

A christian once led a young lady to Christ in an international airport. He had no christian literature with him except a book by the intellectual, Francis Schaeffer called "The God who is There". It was a "heavy-going" book but he gave it to her.

Half an hour later she was pouring over the book in a jet when another gentleman approached her. He enquired about the book she was reading and if she understood it. After some conversation he asked her how long she had been a christian. "Oh!", she replied, "just half an hour!". "Well", replied the gentleman, "let me tell you my name. My name is Francis Schaeffer!" He set to explaining some of the deep and wonderful truths which he had written in his book. Coincidence?

December 13th

"A time to weep ..." Ecclesiastes 3:4

A lady approached me after a service and said something I have never forgotten. She said that when he husband had died she had wept a lot and some fellow christians had told her she was letting the Lord down with her weeping. What a terrible thing to say and what an incredible view of the Lord!

Abraham wept, so did Esau, Joseph, the Children of Israel, Ruth, David, Nehemiah, Job and Jeremiah. Mary and Martha wept and Jesus wept along with them. Tears are given to express grief and it is important that when we face grief we should let our tears flow.

Don't you think, though, there are more tears shed over fictitious tragedies on TV and in cinemas than in our churches over real ones?

December 14th

"A time to laugh ..." Ecclesiastes 3:4

Ian Barclay tells the story about the man who was a visiting speaker at a local church. As he shook hands with his congregation a little man in a grey coat approached and said "You were terrible, today". The man then went out the front door, round the back and in by a side door and rejoined the queue shaking hands with the preacher once more. "You read your notes and what you read was not worth reading", he said. He repeated this strange process quite a few times making comments like "You are a liberal and we are not having you back" and "You shouted too loud" etc.

"I enjoyed coming here", said the preacher to one of the church leaders, "but, tell me, who was the little man in the grey coat?" "Oh! Don't worry about him", was the reply, "he is simple in the head and only repeats what he hears everyone else saying!"

December 15th

"A time to keep silence and a time to speak." Ecclesiastes 3:7

We shall never forget the conversion of George Cowan.

George was teaching children abseiling at a camp for about 500 boys and girls. He taught a few adults, too, and as he let my friend Val English over the edge of a cliff, safely harnessed, Val spoke to him about putting his trust in Christ as Saviour.

A few mornings later at a prayer meeting in the camp, George rose to pray. I've never heard a prayer like it in my life as George told the Lord of his need of salvation and repented toward God and put faith in the Lord Jesus, publicly, and, on the spot! It was a morning of mornings for us all, and, as for his good wife, she was like one that dreamed! Val found the right time to speak a word of witness that day; you may not be on the edge of a cliff but let the gospel loose today when the opportunity arises.

December 16th

"A time to gain and a time to lose." Ecclesiastes 3:6

Our children are a gain. They teach us more than ten thousand seminars ever could. Raising them, I know, is not an easy task and it brings demands that nothing else will. It's a bit like the girl who rebelled against her mother's authority and in the morning her mother found a note on the breakfast table which read; "Dear Mother, I hate you, love Lynda!" The time will come, though, when you have to let your children go. They will leave the nest. Let us remember that children were never designed to be the weld that holds the home together. If the parental relationship has become stronger than the marriage relationship the child has been put into a role it was never designed to fill. Divorce rates skyrocket when the children leave home. Make sure such a thing doesn't happen to you.

"He has made everything beautiful in its time." Ecclesiastes 3:11

The Lord delayed to visit the disciples on the lake until the storm was at its worst. The Lord delayed to go to Jairus's daughter until she was dead. The Lord delayed to go to Lazarus until his body was decomposed.

In the first instance, the disciples learned that Christ had power over nature when he eventually came and stilled the water. Jairus learned that Christ did not only have power over disease but had power over death itself when he eventually raised his daughter. Mary and Martha discovered that Christ had power not only over death but over decomposition when he raised Lazarus from the grave. God sometimes seems to draw a straight line in our lives with a crooked stick but he makes everything beautiful in its time. God's timing is perfect; his delays are not a disappointment. Don't panic.

December 18th

"He has put eternity in their hearts." Ecclesiastes 3:11

See that big hunk of a fellow in your office who curses and blasphemes all day long?; God has put eternity in his heart. See that girl you know who is discontented, who is disinterested in the gospel and seems to care only for this world; God has put eternity in her heart.

I do not wish to be trite but here is a young fellow heading for a wall in an accident with his motorcycle; does he cry, as he faces death, "Oh! Mick Jagger!" Does he cry "Oh! Madonna or The Sting or Betty Boo?" He cries "Oh God!" Why? Because God has put eternity in his heart. Whether

President or King, whether clerk or executive, whether rich or poor, all people think about eternity and we have the message to help them face it without fear. Tell them of the Lord Jesus, today.

December 19th

"I know that whatever God does, it shall be forever. Nothing can be added to it and nothing taken from it. God does it, that man should fear before him." Ecclesiastes 3:14

As Christmastime pervades the Western world you are faced with one clear reality; presents for last year won't do for this year! Impermanence even touches your Christmas tree lights! Sadness also fills many hearts at this time of year because loved ones' seats will be empty.

Let me pose a simple question; when God gives something, does something, can his work be undone? When he sent his Son to Bethlehem and Calvary and offers salvation to all who trust in the Saviour, could a person lose that salvation, once promised, once they've got it? The Bible tells us that the gift of God is eternal life through Jesus Christ our Lord. If it were possible for a person to lose their salvation then God would have to reverse the transaction and take back his gift, wouldn't he? What God does is for ever. When God give eternal life it is for keeps. It's a promise.

December 20th

"Two are better than one because they have a good reward for their labours. For, if they fall one will lift his companion. But woe to him who is alone when he falls for he has no one to help him up." Ecclesiastes 4:9-10

How easy it would have been for Joseph to abandon Mary when he heard the news of the coming virgin birth! Yet, he believed God and cared for and protected her. How easy it would have been for the famous New Testament couple, Aquila and Priscilla to have split when the emperor's nasty edict cast them out of Rome. They stayed together and became a powerful king-pin in the spirit of the New Testament church.

How easy it would have been for Paul to abandon Apollos out of sheer jealousy. They are not put together as friends by many who read Scripture because so many people wanted to make them rivals. "I planted", Paul says, "and Apollos was the water carrier and God gave the increase". To enjoy friends you need more in common with them than just hating the same people. Don't you?

December 21st

"Better is a poor and wise youth than an old and foolish king who will be admonished no more." Ecclesiastes 4:13

Herod was a fool. He knew very well that the child of Bethlehem, poor and all as he was would, one day, establish his kingdom of which there would be no end. Love of power, love of immediate pleasure and political position blinded him to the wisdom of bowing to Christ's lordship.

Thomas Hardy the novelist grew old, saddened by life and its seeming hopelessness. After a great cathedral service he wrote of how he found the christian faith presented as mere "fantasies" and could see no hope in what it was teaching. He regretted his unbelief and asks if "a bird deprived of wings will go earth-bound wilfully"? If you are a young person, happy in your christian faith, be glad. Millions of old men of brilliance die without it.

December 22nd

"As he came from his mother's womb, naked shall he return, to go as he came; and he shall take nothing from his labour which he may carry away in his hand." Ecclesiastes 5:15

My friend was sent to check if the incinerator was working at the crematorium. In the ashes of a body he found a "threepenny bit". "One thing is for sure", he said to the crematorium director, "you can't take it with you".

Morbid? Yes, but true. How lovely to know that when the little baby of Bethlehem was born he didn't fit today's description of man. He was different, for when his time came to leave this earth he led captivity captive and gave gifts to men. What does that mean? It means that he, the God-man, defeated Satan's power in his death and took his spoils and used them to his glory. People who once lived selfish lives now live for Him and others. Why, the best news the world ever had came from a graveyard!

December 23rd

"It is better to go to the house of mourning than to go to the house of feasting, for that is the end of all men; and the living will take it to heart." Ecclesiastes 7:2

All over the country, tonight, people will be feasting. Hotels will be booked out with special functions, restuarants will be packed to the door. "It's Christmas", they will tell you. As I stood watching all the Santaclaustaphobia one day I said to a person standing nearby, "It's far removed from the original story, isn't it?" "And", she replied, quietly, "what was that?"

In these days of feasting today's text says a very startling thing. It says it is better to go to a funeral than a feast. Notice it doesn't say it is wrong to go to a feast but it does say it is better to go to a funeral. Why? Because it will remind you of the brevity of life and where your true priorities lie. When your heart is touched with sorrow you realise that the little baby of Bethlehem came to bear your griefs and carry your sorrows and can turn them into joy. The feasting will be over in the morning. His joy is forever.

December 24th

"The end of a thing is better than its beginning." Ecclesiastes 7:8

There never was a human life which began in the way Christ's began. The more you think about it the more staggering it gets. The helpless little human baby who lay in the manger at Bethlehem, who had to be fed and learn how to talk like any other child was God, in human flesh. "Glory to God in the highest and on earth peace, goodwill toward men", said the heavenly hosts. What a beginning!

Our text tells us that the end is better than the beginning. How could the sweat, the pain, the agony, the blood and the darkness of Calvary be better than the sweetness and the beauty of his birth? Let me put the answer in the form of a question; How could you worship, in a world of pain, a God who is immune to it? The Lord Jesus suffered for us and the cross is our glory. As Edward Shillito has said;

> "The other gods were strong; thou was't weak,
> They rode, but thou did'st stumble to a throne;
> But to our wounds only God's wounds can speak,
> And not a god has wounds, but thou alone."

"For that which is far off and exceedingly deep, who can find it out?" Ecclesiastes 7:

I was invited by a Korean banker to his home for a meal, once. He had come to hear me preach the gospel and found the gospel very confusing. "I go to the Buddhist temple", he said, as I knelt at his sumptuously spread table in Soeul city. "I go after a busy day at the bank and I think of Buddhist teaching and I have peaceful thoughts. I can identify with Buddha because he admits in his writings that he is a sinner. The same goes for Confucius. But you christians, you tell me I am a sinner and that I must get to know a sinless Saviour. It is impossible, if I am a sinner and he is sinless; how get I get to know him?" It is a good question. Is there an answer? There certainly is.

Let me remind you, this Christmas day, of a little girl whose father had left home. Love between him and his wife had gone out the window. When the child took very ill the doctors pled that her father be brought to her hospital bedside. When he arrived he sat down at one side of the bed and would not speak to his wife at the other side. Seeing the situation the little girl put out one hand and took her father's hand and reaching out with her other hand she took her mother's hand and brought both hands together, clutching them tightly over her little chest. As she did so, she died. Do you think it was impossible to reconcile those parents? No. They were reconciled to each other by the death of their daughter. So, says the Bible, "We are reconciled to God through the death of His Son". Have you put your hand in the hand of the man who died for you at Calvary? Why not do it this very Christmas Day? If you do, it will be the happiest one you have ever known.

"Do not take to heart everything people say, lest your hear your servant cursing you. For many times, also, your own heart has known that even you have cursed others." Ecclesiastes 7:21-22

There are a lot of rows in homes over Christmas. People say things they should never say at dinner tables and around the fireside. The walls have ears and maybe you've got to hear what they said about you. Today's test is saying to you "Don't take it all to heart". If you heard everything everybody said about you and took it to heart you would probably never say another word to anyone again or even venture out your own front door!

Our text would remind us of the times when we too have said things about other people and it's a mercy it didn't come to their ears. We didn't mean the half of it, anyway. So, don't upset yourself by what they say about you. A thick skin is a gift from God. Ask him for it, this Christmas! P.S. Stones and sticks are only thrown at fruit bearing trees, aren't they?

"Though a sinner does evil a hundred times, and his days are prolonged, yet I surely know that it will be well with those who fear God." Ecclesiastes 8:12

"It will be well". Though nations war, though the wicked dominate, though crime rampages, though truth is often obscure and the liar seems to reign, and though evil men are not "in trouble as other men, therefore pride serves as their necklace, violence covers them like a garment. Their eyes bulge with abundance; they have more than heart could wish"; their end will come. "It will be well", christian, "it will be well". Those who fear God don't dominate world news now, but, one day they will when they reign with Christ in his coming Kingdom (See 1 Thessalonians 4:14-17; Matthew 25:31-32; Revelation 20:5-6. Go on, look them up!)

No one gets to heaven because he is poor or to hell because he is rich but to those who know Christ as Saviour, it will be well. It's a promise.

December 28th

"The race is not to the swift, nor the battle to the strong, nor bread to the wise, nor riches to men of understanding, nor favour to men of skill but time and chance happens to them all." Ecclesiastes 9:11

The little boy who couldn't understand why God put so many vitamins in spinach and didn't put more of them in ice-cream had a pretty good idea that things just don't work out like you would think they would!

I mean, you would think the most powerful army would win all the battles but look at Vietnam. You would think people of sense and understanding would be people of substance but our teachers are often the poorest paid professionals in the nation. You'd think the most skilled would be in management but often they spend their days in obscurity and less skilled people, lead.

God's sovereignty and timing (here called "chance"), reigns. Don't trust in public relations men or business management gurus for true success. Trust in the Lord with all your heart and He will direct your paths. There is no greater promise. If you know it, you will know true success.

December 29th

"Dead flies putrefy the perfumers ointment and cause it to give off a foul odour; so does a little folly to one respected for wisdom and honour." Ecclesiastes 10:1

So, you got some "Giorgio" for Christmas, or "Paris" or some "Estee Lauder" or some "Chanel" perfume. Lovely. I bought my wife some very special perfume for a special occasion last June and do you know what? She told me she was saving it for Christmas because it was so special!

If dead flies get into your special Christmas perfume, I wouldn't give much for it, would you? It's just like a foolish action in the life of a person long known for their wisdom and honour. A lack of foresight, a failure to realise that consequences of a stupid act before it occurs, a selfish move, a failure to run from even "the very appearance of evil" can ruin a reputation. The lovelier a life the more a foolish action in that life is highlighted. Keep close to Christ and His word and people will see Him in you. God is lovely because God is holy. Holiness is loveliness. So, be holy.

December 30th

"Cast your bread upon the waters, for you will find it after many days." Ecclesiastes 11:1

I love the story Dr. Billy Graham told before 70,000 people in the middle of a thunderstorm at Wembley Stadium recently. He spoke of how he boarded the Royal Yacht Britannia, one day, to dine with the Queen and President Reagan. As he went up the gangway the Royal Naval Officer on the gangway said to him, quietly, as he passed, "Wembley

'55, Sir". In 1955 in bucketing rain, night after night, Dr. Graham had cast Gospel seed. 34 years later on board the Royal Yacht Britannia he found the seed still growing!

For months I have been closeted away, alone with God, writing this little book. In Irish rain and through a New Zealand winter I have sought to cast my bread upon the waters. I know I shall find it again. If it feeds you, I will be overjoyed. My life will have been worth living.

December 31st

"Let us hear the conclusion of the whole matter; Fear God and keep His commandments, for this is the whole duty of man. For God will bring every work into judgment, including every secret thing, whether it is good or whether it is evil." Ecclesiastes 12:13

The wisdom of Solomon has been our companion for a year. It has taught us a lifestyle, under God, that is so different to the lifestyle of the world around us. We have found that these wonderful truths Solomon has driven home to our hearts are, in fact available to everyone. But how does he sum it all up? What are his famous last words? We will all, he says, face the judgment of God and give an account of how we have lived. How can we, then, get ready for that incredible moment when we shall stand face to face with God? He concludes that we must "fear God and keep his commandments". How can we do that? By trusting Christ as Saviour and Lord and seeking to live for his glory. He will give us power to live as Solomon has said we can. For, after all, as the Lord Jesus said of himself "A greater than Solomon is here". Trust Him. He keeps all his promises.